The Teaching of Reading

The Teaching of Reading

DONALD MOYLE

Senior Lecturer in Education
Tutor to the one year in-service course
leading to the Diploma in the Teaching of Reading
Edge Hill College of Education

WARD LOCK EDUCATIONAL

o 7062 3123 6 hardback
o 7062 3124 4 paperback
First published 1968
Reprinted 1969
Second edition 1970
Reprinted 1970, 1971
Third edition 1972
Reprinted 1972

Set in 12 point Monotype Bembo
Printed by The Garden City Press Limited
Letchworth, Hertfordshire, SG6 1JS
for Ward Lock Educational Limited
116 Baker Street, London W1M 2BB

Contents

Preface to first edition

This book has been written specifically for students in colleges of education and teachers who find themselves insufficiently equipped to teach reading as well as they would wish.

I have endeavoured to provide the psychological and historical background and review current issues in order that the teacher will be able to make her own decisions regarding methods and materials. There is no attempt to push a particular method and though some examples of practical work are given these could be used in conjunction with almost any approach or materials.

One plea is made throughout, namely that the teacher will always base instruction on a knowledge of the child's personal maturity and then proceed to plan growth in experience and attainment in a scientific, yet interesting and vital manner.

Preface to third edition

The speed of change in education continues to gain momentum yet still the cry is heard that the standards of attainment of our children and their attitudes to and interest in reading is seemingly unchanged.

Because of changes in educational thinking and the expansion of our understanding of the reading process it has been necessary to make quite extensive revisions of the original text. Essential though a thorough knowledge of the early stages undoubtedly is, children need help throughout their school life if they are to develop into effective readers. Accordingly more space has been given to the development of comprehension and the use of reading.

So often faith for the future has been placed in new materials for the children. Now more than ever before we realize that the understanding and expertise of the teacher is the more important factor in gaining real success for the children. I hope that this book will contribute to a greater understanding of the reading task.

Donald Moyle 1972

Acknowledgments

The field of reading is well chronicled and I have therefore been able to draw on a vast store of experience and experiment which has appeared in print in the past. I am most grateful to a number of people who have allowed me to quote from their work, particularly Professor M. D. Vernon, Dr J. M. Morris, Professor D. Durrell, Professor W. S. Gray, Messrs A. E. Tansley and R. H. Nicholls.

I wish to thank Mr R. G. Cave who originally suggested that I should write the book, and the following people whose comments on the first edition were most helpful, Misses E. Cobb and E. Hulme, Mrs L. M. Moyle, Messrs A. Bessell, S. Jackson, L. Litt, J. A. S. Richardson and S. H. Wrench.

Many people have given valuable advice since the first edition was published and I would particularly like to thank Dr J. M. Morris, Professor J. E. Merritt and Geoffrey Roberts together with the teachers who have joined me at Edge Hill College over the past seven years for intensive study of the reading process.

Introduction by Joyce M. Morris

The Teaching of Reading is a much needed book when considered in the following context.

There is some evidence that the reading standards of the school population have improved steadily since the Second World War. Nevertheless, the progress made gives no grounds for complacency, since it is estimated that about ten per cent of school leavers cannot read well enough to cope with the ordinary day to day demands of life in our traditionally 'literate' society. Recent research also indicates that at the other end of the scale of reading potentiality, a sizeable proportion of undergraduates have not sufficiently mastered the more complex reading skills to enable them to complete a degree course. Reading disability of one kind or another is therefore a matter for concern in Britain.

Investigations conducted by the NFER suggest that, although unfavourable personal attributes and home circumstances play an important part in preventing individuals from realizing their full reading potential, adverse school conditions are at least equally responsible. These adverse conditions are not confined to the material aspects of educational provision which can only be radically improved when greater financial resources are available than in the present economic situation. They include inadequacies in the teaching of reading which I am not alone in thinking could be remedied by three related types of action.

First, a great step forward would be made if priority was given to the teaching of reading when pre-service courses for teachers are planned. For obvious reasons a reasonable amount of time is usually allocated to this important subject in courses for those intending to teach infants. It is not yet as widely recognized that at least as much time should be devoted to training prospective junior and secondary teachers to meet the challenge of ensuring growth for backward readers. They must also be equipped to develop reading skills beyond the stage of getting literal meaning from print.

Even those colleges of education which have got their priorities right cannot be expected to produce teachers of reading with sufficient theoretical knowledge and practical experience to be entirely successful in the immediate tasks that lie ahead. A second step forward therefore would be to make it standard practice for newly qualified teachers to attend appropriate in-service courses on 'the first R'.

Finally, it is highly desirable that British universities, like those in other countries, should make it possible for experienced teachers to take advanced courses leading to an academic diploma or degree in reading or 'language arts'. Granted this and greater opportunities to conduct reading research at a professional level, all those responsible for the pre-service and in-service training of tomorrow's teachers of reading could have the necessary 'specialist' knowledge for their task in addition to successful classroom experience.

Meanwhile, literature in the field of reading remains almost the sole source of expert guidance for a high proportion of students, practising teachers and teacher trainers in Britain. It is unfortunate therefore that relatively little of the vast amount published is relevant to their needs. Much of the material is written by and for research workers, in that it assumes in the reader a knowledge of scientific method and statistics. Moreover, the majority of authoritative books specifically for the teaching profession are by foreign authors, with the result that the references and advice given are not strictly relevant in our educational context. The comparatively small number of books of this kind by British writers are concerned mainly with teaching infants to read and/or the problems of reading backwardness.

Mr Moyle has set out to provide a basic book containing the information which is essential for teachers to promote reading growth at *every* stage of development. He is also one of the few British educationists who have combined knowledge from a comprehensive, critical and up to date review of research with suggestions for putting it into practice in a variety of circumstances with pupils of different types and ages.

The Teaching of Reading has many other qualities besides being a sound practical guide. In my opinion the most striking feature is its balanced approach to all the main issues involved. Controversial questions such as the influence of heredity and environment on the acquisition of reading skills and the validity of the concept of 'reading readiness' are discussed in a scholarly manner, taking into

9

account relevant research findings. There is however no deference to scientific inquiry because of its status; where conclusive evidence is lacking the author comes down heavily on the side of common sense. He also considers every problem fairly from the angle of the child and the teacher.

Another notable feature of this book is that, whilst drawing attention to all that is best in modern practice, it underlines the dangers of too great a reliance on discovery methods and incidental learning. We are reminded that reading is a product of civilization not, like physical growth, a natural phenomenon. Hence, children generally will neither begin to learn to read nor proceed to acquire the necessary reading skills if left to their own devices no matter how rich the reading environment provided by their teachers. They must be given systematic instruction based on an accurate diagnosis of their individual needs throughout their school lives.

By making this the central theme of his book, Mr Moyle has shown courage at a time when an educationist who even uses the word 'instruction' is liable to be classed as a reactionary. He has done so in accordance with the findings of recent research, my own included, and in the interests of children. This is what makes his contribution so admirable and important.

A final word. I am convinced that if this book is studied as widely and as deeply as it deserves to be, and if its principles are put into practice, it will help greatly to improve the teaching of reading thereby bringing nearer the day when reading disability of one kind or another is no longer a matter for concern in Britain.

April 1968

Glossary

Some of the more technical terms used in the book are listed below in alphabetical order. The definitions given are those which the author had in mind when using the words in the text though no doubt many will permit of a wider application.

aetiology	the study of the causes of a disability e.g. backwardness.
analysis	a breaking down to simple elements e.g. a word into its individual letter sounds.
antonym	a word of opposite meaning to a given word.
attainment	the level of accomplishment reached in a given subject.
auditory acuity	sensitivity or sharpness of hearing.
auditory discrimination	the power to detect differences and similarities in sound images.
auditory memory	concerning the ability to remember a sound which has been perceived.
auditory perception	mental awareness of a sound sensation.
babbling	sounds uttered by the baby, not true speech but a preparation for it.
backward	a general term used to describe a child whose attainment is well below that of the average child in his age group.
blending	the mental act of linking together the constituent sounds of a word to form the whole word.
cerebral damage	damage to the brain.
cerebral dominance	the leading hemisphere of the brain which appears to determine hand and eye preference.
cloze procedure	a technique used for testing reading attainment and the level of difficulty of books. Words are deleted or omitted by selecting every nth (e.g. every tenth)

word or by the use of a table of random numbers. The child being tested is required to select an appropriate word to fill the space.

cognitive
describing intellectual activity, knowing as opposed to feeling.

compensatory activity
a task designed to overcome any given weakness in a child by the use of some other skill or ability to achieve the same ends.

comprehension
the skill of reading to extract knowledge or reading with understanding.

concept
an idea, usually signified by a word which has been formed by the mental classification and generalization of experience.

controlled vocabulary
a book in which the introduction of new words is limited to prevent the child having too great a load of new material to memorize.

cornea
the protective membrane at the front of the eye.

correlation
the relationship between two sets of test scores by the same group of people. Statistically a perfect relationship would yield a correlation of plus 1·0, complete lack of relationship would be 0 and the exact opposite minus 1·0.

crossed laterality
a lack of established dominance among the eyes and limbs, e.g. a left-handed person who is right-eyed.

deprivation
a lack of normal human experience.

diacritical
the use of a system of marks to guide the reader to the correct sound value of the symbol.

diagnosis
the search for strengths and weaknesses within a child and the possible causes in order to improve the child's rate of progress.

digraphs
two letters, vowel or consonant which combine to make one sound.

diphthongs	two vowels representing one vowel sound.
dyslexia	difficulty in reading and perception believed to result from damage to the brain or a lack of maturity of the neurological mechanisms.
eye movements	the description of the manner in which the eyes traverse a line of print.
eyedness	referring to the preferred or leading eye.
fixation	the focusing of the eye upon a word or group of words.
flash cards	words or sentences placed upon cards which are briefly exposed before the child to encourage speedy word recognition.
fluency	the ability to read without hesitancy.
general ability	an aspect of mental capacity which appears to have an influence in the performance of all tasks.
gestalt	form, structure or integrated whole.
graded reading scheme	a series of books which are arranged in order of difficulty.
handedness	concerning the preferred hand.
homonym	a word with the same spelling as another but with a different meaning.
hyperactivity	excessive and often uncontrolled movements.
illiterate	unable to read—statistically usually refers to a person of 15 or more years who has not attained the reading standard of the normal child of 7 years.
inner speech	the act of speaking inwardly as one reads. The activity is usually accompanied by slight vibration of the vocal organs.
intelligence	mental capacity or mental activity.
intelligence quotient	a measure of mental capacity obtained by testing. The ratio of mental age to chronological age expressed as a percentage.
inversion	in reading this term is usually reserved for the act of seeing a letter upside down.

ita	initial teaching alphabet.
kinaesthetic	perception obtained through the sense of touch and movement.
language experience approach	an approach to the teaching of reading which is based in the child's own experiences, all vocabulary used being drawn at first from his own spoken words and later from his written work.
language facility	ability to use words intelligently.
linguistic development	the growth of ability to understand words and of sensitivity to meaning and sentence construction.
linguistic method	an approach to the teaching of reading wherein words are graded according to the complexity of their spelling.
logographic	a system of writing in which each word in a language has its own symbol as opposed to alphabetical writing wherein words may have symbols in common.
maturation	the process of growth as opposed to the process of learning.
mechanical reading attainment	level of achievement in the recognition of words without the aid of context.
medium	the characters used in written language.
mental age	an assessment of intelligence expressed in relation to the intelligence graded by age of the total population.
mixed handedness	lack of an established preference for the use of one hand over the other.
mixed methods	an approach to the teaching of reading wherein a number of methods are employed e.g. phonic, look/say and sentence method.
motivation	the incentive to pursue a particular task.
non-verbal tests	tests of intelligence which do not employ language as a medium.
orally	expressed by word of mouth.
orientation	the chosen direction, in English that of reading from left to right along a line of print.

parallel schemes	the equating of books of equal difficulty and similar vocabulary.
perception	awareness of the stimulation of a sense organ.
performance tests	tests of practical or concrete ability which usually avoid the use of language.
phonetic	a language is said to be phonetic when there is perfect consistency between sound and symbol.
phonic methods	an approach to reading instruction where the emphasis is placed upon the sound value of letters as a means of word recognition.
pictogram	a device used by early man where the picture represented some incident or thought.
primer	an early or first reading book.
readability	the level of ease or difficulty of a given text.
readability formulae	formulae used in the calculation of the level of difficulty of a text. The most common measures employed are those of word and sentence length.
readiness	the level of development necessary to embark successfully on a new learning task.
reading age	an individual's attainment in reading expressed as the reading standard for the average child. Thus a child of ten years scoring 30 words on Schonell's test would be deemed to be reading at the level of the average child of eight years.
reading/thinking activities	strategies employed to encourage the reader to read with expectancy and anticipate the author's thoughts.
remedial work	tasks designed to enable a child whose attainment level is unsatisfactory to make greater progress.
repetition rate	the number of times a word is repeated in any given text.

retarded	descriptive of a child whose attainment falls below his ability.
retina	the section of the eye which receives the visual sensation.
reversal	the turning of a letter or word e.g. d for b or was for saw.
scanning	glancing speedily over a text to find specific items of information.
semi-literate	a reader who has not attained fluency. Statistically someone of a reading age between 7 and 9 years.
skimming	a method of reading quickly in order to gain the gist of a passage or to locate a particular section.
specific abilities	specific as against general in that they enter into certain and not all tasks.
standardized	a test is said to be standardized when it has been administered to a representative population and its consistency and validity have proved satisfactory.
synonym	a word whose meaning is identical to another given word.
synthesis	the linking together of constituent sounds to form the whole word.
tachistoscope	a device for controlling the length of time a flash card is displayed.
traditional orthography	the usual spelling of words in English.
validity	the extent to which a test measures the area it purports to test.
verbal ability	the ability to use language intelligently.
verbal tests	tests which involve the use of language or seek to find the level of language development.
visual acuity	quality and sharpness of vision.
visual discrimination	the ability to detect differences and similarities in size, shape and colour.
visual memory	the ability to recall a visual image.
visual perception	mental awareness of an image which falls on the retina.
vocabulary	the number of words a child can use or, in reading, recognize in print.

WISC	Weschler Intelligence Scale for Children.
word blindness	inability to perceive or memorize the printed word.
word building	the building up of a word from its constituent letters or sounds.
word recognition	the ability to recognize a word in print.

PART ONE

The historical, linguistic and psychological
background to the learning
and teaching of reading

CHAPTER 1

Language and reading

Reading and writing are forms of communication, as is gesture, but, unlike gesture, they are both entirely based in our spoken language. It is essential, therefore, that an understanding of the process of learning to read should be preceded by an understanding of the total language situation and the use we make of language, not only as a communication art, but also as the vehicle of our thought processes.

It has been said that the formulation of language is mankind's greatest accomplishment, yet, as far as we can ascertain, from the very earliest times men have been able to communicate in some form of speech. The most primitive and isolated tribes have developed this skill, even though the peculiar system of tongue-clicking employed by some tribes of Pygmies would seem to be very far removed from the sophisticated language which we employ.

We can only surmise how speech first came to be employed, but it would seem logical that its origin was in the emotional cry—those expressions of fear, pain and ecstasy which are involuntarily uttered when strong emotions are aroused. By virtue of the type of cry and intonation used, the hearer is able to interpret the emotion which has given rise to the cry, but cannot interpret from the cry itself the circumstances, the cause, nor the action required to satisfy the emotional or physical need. Sound and intonation were no doubt accompanied by gesture, facial expression and bodily movement, and this would enable the hearer to gain much more information concerning the total situation. Many animals are successfully trained to respond to this type of intonation and gesture and anyone who has observed a performance of mime given by Marcel Marceau will realize how extensive is the information which can be expressed through this medium. Gesture is undoubtedly superior to the emotional cry as a form of communication and the two together can be most expressive. There are limitations still, for gesture, though it can be used to portray objects, actions, even emotions, cannot be extended to cater for the more general and abstract ideas which we can express in our language today and, of course, it is also very easily misinterpreted. Gesture too would be a very clumsy vehicle of thought for if in our reflections we had to visualize the total action or emotion, thought would be a laborious, unwieldy and inaccurate activity.

The use of sentences and later the division of sentences into individual words no doubt grew quickly from the limitations of the communication media we have just described for man is a social creature and feels a need to communicate his desires, feelings and thoughts to others. Thus language grew from social contact which brought wider social contact and in turn this widening of social activities demanded further growth of language skills.

Language has also contributed greatly to the progress made by mankind by providing, not only the external social skill of communication, but also by giving man an advanced type of shorthand which has enabled him to communicate with himself in thought. Words could now be used as labels to symbolize the objects of his environment, and concepts could be made and named so that he was now able to classify and memorize his experiences more easily. As he progressed, man was able to solve problems and reach forward to new developments and inventions, an act which could never have been possible had he been limited in his thought processes to visual images of the objects of his environment.

This theoretical reconstruction of the historical growth of language, which has been very briefly set out above, has a parallel in the development of language skills among our own children. The young child passes through the stage of the emotional cry when he expresses the comfort and discomfort cries of babyhood. At an early age he begins to babble, to experiment with the range of sounds which he is capable of making, and very soon he has uttered and practised the whole range of sounds which are necessary to speak our language. The young child is capable of innovation and will make up his own names for items of his environment which have special meaning or attraction for him but, fortunately, he is born into a world with a ready made language and therefore the next stage in his development is speeded up, in comparison to that of early man, by imitation of the speech of those around him. He is able to compare and equalize his own vocalization, in response to any given stimulus, to that of his mother or elder brothers and sisters.

The child also progresses through similar stages in his use of language. His first words are usually nouns and this corresponds to the labelling stage where he explores his environment and learns to apply a particular sound to any given object. Next in time comes the use of verbs as the child gains an appreciation of actions, followed closely by pronouns as he learns to distinguish himself from the objects of his environment. Some people believe that our reading instruction should follow this pattern of speech development so that the first exposure to the printed word would be limited to the recognition of nouns and other parts of speech would follow in the sequence in which they originally appeared. However, by the time the child enters school at 5 years his speech, though still characterized by the excessive use of nouns, includes most other parts of speech and thus this return to an earlier stage would seem unnecessary. It is perhaps sufficient that most of our primers, acknowledging the content of the speech of young children concentrate their attention upon nouns which label objects commonly found in the environment of the young child.

Written language

Historically, spoken language was developed before written language and in a similar way our children must learn to respond to oral communication before we can attempt to teach them to read. The invention of language presented in a written form was yet another immense step forward in man's progress. Before this innovation, all information had to be passed on by word of mouth. Stories, facts and the accrued wisdom of any one generation depended on it being memorized and transmitted through speech by each successive generation to the following one. This, out of necessity, decreed that human progress would be slow, facts were often distorted and discoveries and inventions were sometimes lost to future generations. With the advent of written language the keeping of permanent records became possible and the storehouse of human experience was increased. No longer was the communication of knowledge limited to a small group of contemporaries; now a man's work could be transmitted to a wider audience both within and beyond his own generation. More than this, knowledge could now be communicated more fully and with less likelihood of inaccuracy and misinterpretation.

Written language appears to have grown from man's desire to record those things which seemed important to him and probably started with the notched stick of the trader and wall drawings depicting the outstanding prowess of a hunter or a great feat in battle, such as have been discovered in the caves used for shelter by our distant ancestors. These pictures, however, were not written language but did originate from the same basic desire to record. In order of time they were probably followed by the pictogram which was the first real attempt to present language in a written form. Here the same order was used as in speech, and pictures were symbolically used as when the picture of the moon represented the passage of a month of time. The next step forward was an attempt to use a graphic signal to represent a word and our numerals are of this order. One can see, however, that a system of writing which had a separate graphic signal for every different word in the language would present a tremendous task for any child attempting to learn to read or write that language. The people of China are at the moment working to modify their own script which is still largely logographic in character in order to reduce the forty thousand or so different signals of which it is composed.

To overcome these difficulties, certain tribes in the ancient world devised a system of writing where the syllables of words were represented by a single sign. The Minoans and Sumerians had highly developed systems of this type more than 3,000 years before the birth of Christ and the Japanese script of today is formed partially in this manner.

Our written language is based on the Greco-Roman alphabet, and alphabetical writing is the most modern stage in the development of written language and became possible because some words had certain sounds in common and these sounds could therefore be represented by a common symbol. Some languages have an almost complete correspondence between sound and alphabetical symbol but alas such a consistency has not been present in the language of our own country since the tenth century. At the best we can only claim a 40 per cent consistency and teachers faced with the task of inducting young children into the mysteries of reading often sigh for a more consistent sound/symbol relationship. Such thoughts have given rise to many attempts to reform the spelling of English but to date none have come anywhere near gaining the support needed to make such a step possible. Nevertheless, teachers in many parts of the English speaking world are experimenting with more consistent alphabets, such as i t a and Unifon in the hope that the initial stages of reading may be made less irksome for the child.

Historically, therefore, writing must have preceded reading and some authorities, notably Montessori, have suggested that we should teach our children to write before we expect them to read. Some others, e.g. Fries, assert that the true, and by far the most used, basic skill is reading and that writing should be ignored until some attainment in reading has been achieved. Most teachers feel that it is helpful to the child to commence reading and writing together. The reasons for this practice are twofold. Young children love to create, to perform and to practise. To delay writing therefore would be to deny them one form of expression. Secondly, the two activities are complementary to one another and therefore consolidation of reading progress can be gained through written work.

What is reading?
Writing is the process of presenting speech in a more permanent visual form and therefore reading can be looked upon as the reverse of this process, namely, turning the collection of symbols seen upon a piece of paper into 'talk', or, in the case of silent reading, into an image of speech sounds. This in English means gaining the ability to read from left to right and from top to bottom of the page, the recognition of letter symbols and their grouping into words.

In the *Second Report of the National Committee on Reading* (1937) W. S. Gray wrote as follows:

> A broader view of the nature of reading is that it involves the recognition of the important elements of meaning in their essential relations, including accuracy and thoroughness in comprehension. This definition, while implying a thorough mastery of word recognition, attaches major importance to thought getting. The fact should be pointed out, however, that comprehension, as the term is used here, provides merely for a grasp of meaning in the form in which it is presented. It does not include the reader's reaction to the facts or view apprehended nor the discovery of their value or significance. . . .
> The Yearbook Committee believes that any conception of reading that fails to include reflection, critical evaluation, and the clarification of meaning is inadequate.

R. Morris (1963) terms this 'responsive' reading, in that the reader is called upon to make an active mental response to the content of the passage read. The reader is called upon, not only to understand the message of the author, but to reflect upon it, assess its value by comparison with previously learned concepts and finally to reach out in imagination to new realms as a result of the stimulus of the text. It is suggested that if our children learn to use their reading in this way they will not be in danger of losing their individuality under the pressures of modern mass media, nor will the progress of mankind as a whole be stunted.

Morris reviews teaching methods with the purpose of analysing which will be most helpful to gain a growth of 'responsive' reading for our children. On the other hand, Fries (1963) dismissed these supposed higher levels of reading as being items which are separate from the reading process for comprehension, evaluation, imagination and creativity can equally well be practised upon the spoken word. As such he maintains they are not unique to the reading process and therefore not part of it. Thus he sees reading basically, though in fairness, as we shall see in Chapter 5, not entirely, as a matter of learning the skill of responding to the visual symbols of our language in a speedy and automatic fashion and converting these perceptions into language within our mental processes.

It would seem that Fries is correct in saying that the mental processes included in the type of reading Morris has termed 'responsive' are separate from the act of reading itself. However, we must also consider the uses to which our reading is to be put in any analysis of an approach to teaching techniques. If we wish our children to read with understanding, to evaluate and also to think creatively as a result of their reading, must we not encourage these skills from the very beginning? The child must see a purpose in and gain enjoyment from reading from the earliest moments of instruction. Just as mathematical understanding is not fostered by the learning of arithmetical computation alone, the ability to make maximum use of our reading will not come through a training only in the skills of word recognition. Again, the mastery of word recognition is a lengthy process for the child and if he does not experience enjoyment in the medium from the earliest stages he will lack the motivation to use the skill at a later date.

If reading is about the interaction of ideas between author and reader then the child must be encouraged to read in such a manner from the very beginning. He should also see how useful the skill is in the real world by being placed in situations where reading is essential to the completion of the activity. In other words he should read for a purpose—to fulfil his needs. When this happens the child will see reading as relevant and essential to his daily life.

Further reading

FRIES, C. C. (1962) *Linguistics and Reading* Holt, Rinehart and Winston

MORRIS, R. (1962) *Success and Failure in Learning to Read* Oldbourne

WILKINSON, A. (1971) *The Foundations of Language* OUP

CHAPTER 2

A brief history of reading teaching

It is important to view any method of teaching which we employ with some suspicion. We must regularly ask 'Why do I approach this point in this manner?' 'Is this the most appropriate method for this child?' and lastly, 'How can I improve the effectiveness of my teaching?' In our present state of knowledge there is no known correct or perfect way to approach the teaching of reading. Methods which are highly successful with teacher A and children X may not work at all well for teacher B with children Y or with children X. This is because the process of learning to read is such a complex mixture of individual abilities, skills and personality traits. On the one hand the teacher must have a thorough knowledge of the children as individuals and on the other an understanding not only of the techniques involved in various teaching methods, but also of the advantages and disadvantages involved. The teacher would do well therefore to look carefully at the methods available, and the facts, theories and assumptions upon which they are based. For this purpose we turn now to a brief examination of the historical growth of teaching methods and an analysis of the respective strengths and weaknesses of them, drawing from each one that which is considered good and helpful. For convenience we will do this under two general headings—'whole' methods and 'phonic' methods.

At certain stages in educational history some methods of reading teaching have gained special prominence but it must always be borne in mind that practice in the classroom rarely runs hand in hand with current theory. Teachers do not change their approach overnight nor would one desire this to happen. The tendency is more usually a gradual process of grafting new methods on to old and only a minority of teachers completely change their approach. Classroom methods therefore rarely mirror the pure approach advocated or tested by the research worker. Thus although we are considering methods under the two broad headings 'phonic' and 'whole' most teachers have used and continue to use a mixture of approaches from both areas in their classroom practice.

Whole word methods
The story method
Before our language became a written one, a large heritage of myth and legend had been built up by passing stories from generation to generation by word of mouth. No doubt this involved a vast amount of learning by repetition. It is not unnatural therefore that when language became written, learning to read by repetition and memorization was widely used. Many of our folk tales still contain rhythmical repetition which is attractive to the ear of the child and often the sound of the words conjures up a mental picture which acts as a further aid to memorization. Some of our reading schemes make wide use of this approach today, e.g. *Beacon Reading Scheme*, the *Gay Way Books* and the *Beginning to Read Books*.

The following extract is taken from Book 3 of the *Beacon Readers*:

Man won't kill ox,
Ox won't drink water,
Water won't put out fire,
Fire won't burn stick,
Stick won't beat dog,
Dog won't bite pig,
Pig won't go over the stile,
And I shan't get home tonight.

Even more recently (1960) the method has been used widely in the *Beginner Books* published by Collins and Harvill. The following is taken from *Are you my Mother?* by P. D. Eastman:

The kitten was not his mother.
The hen was not his mother.
The dog was not his mother.
So the baby bird went on. Now he came to a cow.

This method was widely used at the end of the eighteenth century when perhaps the most used story was 'The Little Red Hen'. The method paled before an increasing use of phonic techniques and was subjected to severe criticism by Buswell as recently as 1922 on the grounds that the children were in fact learning the story by heart rather than reading it. Certainly we cannot doubt the truth of this for before being given the story in print, it was read over to the children several times and possibly discussed and dramatized. The method limits the possibilities of gaining smooth growth and children soon grow beyond the stage of enjoying such stories.

It is easy to poke fun at this method from our more advanced, albeit far from perfect, knowledge of the growth of reading attainment in children. Nevertheless children did learn to read by this method which means that it must have some advantages to offer. First of all children enjoy a certain amount of rhythm and repetition in their work for it gives them not only enjoyment, but a sense of security in the medium. I have often heard infant teachers expressing the view that a child was merely memorizing the words of a primer and not learning them. It would appear however that many children go through a stage when words can be recognized in the context learned but not elsewhere. This, I am convinced, is a stage in development which some children find helpful to their progress and the teacher should design activities to ensure a natural advancement from this stage rather than take the child to task and make him reread the page over and over again.

Buswell's condemnation was far too sweeping. Many infant school teachers use the method still to great effect with such material as nursery rhymes and whilst no one would suggest that it should be the only way—memorization has a place in the early teaching of reading. Indeed many children learn their first words in print by having them pointed out by parents when reading well-loved and oft-repeated bedtime stories.

Word Patterns

It is strange to think that the word-whole approach to reading is considered by many teachers to be a product of the last three decades, for Comenius advocated this approach to the teaching of reading in the seventeenth century. Like most of the ideas of Comenius this reading method was long ignored and remained little used by teachers until it was given great support by Gestalt psychology although it had been practised fairly widely in America in the nineteenth century under the influence of Webb and had some support in this country in the early part of this century. The Gestalt school of psychology gained prominence in the second, third and fourth decades of this century, but its description of mental activity is no longer acceptable to the majority of psychologists. Nevertheless a number of books concerning the teaching of reading quote Gestalt theory as their support for recommending whole word methods.

The term 'gestalt' loosely interpreted means 'form' and the theory became popular that a word was recognized by the shape presented by the outer contour of the whole group of letters of which it was composed.

Helen P. Davidson (1931), researching into the influence of mental age upon readiness for reading, devised a scheme of teaching words entirely by their shape using the following steps:

1. The child was required to match geometric shapes to the identical shapes outlined on a piece of card.

2. The child, having become proficient at the above now moved to the matching of shapes which represented word outlines

e.g.

= **dog**

= **little**

3. The child now had to distinguish a shape representing his own name from the shapes of the names of the other children in his group.

4. Now for the first time the letters in the word were printed on a card. Starting with his own name the child would then learn the names of the other children in the group.

5. Common objects around the room were now taught in the same manner as above.

6. The children then began to play action games and obey instructions in short sentences, thus reaching the stage of reading sentences without ever having their attention drawn to the fact that words were composed of letters.

Helen Davidson published her results in 1931 and these, together with other similar works, had a great impact upon the teaching of reading in English speaking countries. For many years before this, reading instruction had been almost entirely a process of phonic drill. Many teachers felt that this was unreal and tedious and infant school teachers in particular looked upon the new approach as one which would raise the reading lesson to a level where the children could find real interest and enthusiasm. The tendency grew for teachers to look on words as shapes rather than a number of letters placed in a special order, each having a distinctive sound.

Helen Davidson discovered, however, that although the attention of the children had never been drawn to individual letters, that the children often made mistakes which pointed to the fact that the word was not being memorized by its total shape but often by outstanding characteristics. Her analysis of errors show that children assumed words by initial letters, and mistakes such as the following were made:

'but' might be read for 'butter' or 'little' might be the response to 'light'.

Though stages 1 to 3 of Davidson's approach have rarely been used in this country, the later stages of the method were readily taken over and the look/say approach to reading is still the most widely used method in the infant school classrooms in this country.

The term 'look/say' has come to be closely associated with the work of Gates in America whose first published works on the teaching of reading appeared in the mid twenties. The theory involved in the 'look/say' and 'word pattern' methods is very similar but in the former one rarely sees word shapes considered separately from the letters which compose the word. It would seem to be something of a pretence to say that a shape such as ⌐⌐⌐ should represent a help to unlocking the word 'butter' for it could equally well stand for 'batter' or even 'kitten'. The look/say method, in the form in which we have come to know it, uses actual words from the very beginning, these words being taught by use of pictures, flash cards and the child's experience. The method took on stronger roots as interest in activity methods began to appear, and from the early 1940s many of our infant schools abandoned any attempt at systematic phonic instruction. To the observer it seemed that all that was necessary was to provide the children with attractive books containing well controlled vocabularies and simply hear the children read. This, however, was a complete misunderstanding of the work of Gates and one which brought its own peculiar difficulties. Gates did indeed emphasize the 'wholeness' of words but he did so as the sum of their parts. A casual glance at his own reading scheme reveals in his workbooks, exercises of a nature not greatly different from those in some phonic books—the only difference being that the skill involved in solving them was largely that of visual discrimination whereas previously the discriminatory factor involved was in the realm of sound. The child would be asked to find an identical word to any given word among a number of words whose patterns were very similar, e.g.

Underline the word which is exactly like the first word
big ‖ bag   bog   dig   <u>big</u>   dog

Many authorities on the teaching of reading during the last three decades have recommended that the look/say approach should be used exclusively in the early stages of reading growth; Schonell suggests that quite a sizeable vocabulary should be built up in this way and supplemented by phonic work drawn from words the child can already read, when the child has reached a mental and reading attainment age of from $6\frac{1}{2}$ to 7 years. Were Schonell's recommendations universally true for all children, his suggested approach is limiting, for a child who can read a given word finds little to motivate him to analyse it into its component parts and will often adopt the attitude that this is 'baby stuff'.

Despite the enthusiasm of the 1930s the look/say approach did not prove to be the salvation of all children in the sphere of reading. It did, however, encourage publishers to give more thought to the format and illustrative quality of their reading schemes and started a new flood of research into methods of teaching reading.

Many of the books produced in this wave of enthusiasm have however tended to attract the teacher rather than the child. 'The cat sat on the mat' would after all seem more meaningful than 'Come, come Jane'. In fact, many of the new primers carried a story in the pictures that was but poorly reflected in the text. Two great difficulties had to be overcome, namely, that of presenting the child with sufficient repetition of the words to ensure memorization and that of using words whose general contours could not easily be confused. In the early days these difficulties produced very stilted and unreal texts but some more recent books have solved the problem much more happily. For example, after extensive use of Tansley and Nicholls, *Racing to Read* scheme, I have discovered the repetition to be adequate even for very dull children to memorize the vocabulary and yet not lose interest in the story. However, in Book One of this series it is necessary to point out letter discrimination in order that the pairs of words, 'green' and 'garden', 'wall' and 'window' are not confused.

The above confusion must lead us to question whether in fact this is one which arises from the inability to remember word wholes or whether in fact it arises from children assuming a word from only part of its component letters. Certainly errors of the type 'look' for 'book' and 'caravan' for 'canary' are very evident in the reading of children taught by this method. One can only conclude that some children at least form a habit which is hardly a helpful one, of guessing a word using context plus the first letter, first two letters, first letter and length of word or some other outstanding characteristic. It is often argued that adults read in this way and perhaps there is some truth in this, but it must be remembered that the adult can make much more adequate use of context and by virtue of his greater fixation span can pay more attention to outstanding characteristics. Many young children probably take in only about 3 letters in any one fixation nor have they the same facility for easy progression from left to right. Again if total shape is the aim, a word of six letters may well involve two or three fixations of the eye which creates obvious difficulties to forming a mental image of that word. The method is, of course, predominantly visual and as such must be limiting for those children whose visual processes are not so well developed as in the average child.

Kinaesthetic method

In 1921 a method was formulated which in many respects represents a whole word approach and for which outstanding successes were claimed. This was the Kinaesthetic approach developed in the USA by Fernald and Keller. This method originated in the era when gross difficulty in learning to read was quickly coming to be known as 'word blindness' and attributed to some cerebral damage.

Fernald gathered together in a clinic a number of children who had failed to make any progress in reading under normal school conditions. The schools used predominantly visual and auditory approaches and Fernald decided to experiment with another sense, namely that of touch. The child traced over a word which was presented in cursive writing on a piece of card, the word being spoken aloud as the tracing commenced. This activity continued until the word could be produced from memory. Many words were learned in this way and tracing continued with all new words until they could be recognized in typescript. From this stage writing of the words was encouraged and sentences introduced. For a long period new words met were always treated by commencing the tracing process again. The origins of this method are to be found in Montessori's suggestion that tracing words formed of sandpaper letters was helpful to reading.

The method was originated as a remedial approach for children with difficulty and Schonell commends its use in this context. In some cases Fernald obtained tremendous and speedy improvements but in others the method proved a complete failure, possibly because these children did not have a strong kinaesthetic ability.

The method, however, drew attention to many factors not previously considered with the importance they have deserved. Montessori had suggested that writing should precede reading and whereas many would not accept this, most people today would agree that writing is a very definite aid to word recognition and word memorization and is probably the very best approach to establishing good left/right orientation. Fernald also drew attention to the importance of basing reading instruction upon the existing language development of the child by taking all the material for early work from words and sentences provided by each individual child.

The main criticism of the method is its limited sense appeal which makes it unsuitable for use entirely on its own but it also has the difficulty of being a slow and tedious method. The child having suggested its own word would commence the activity with great enthusiasm but this would quickly wane when the word had to be repeatedly traced sometimes to the order of between 50 and 100 times before instant recognition of it among other words was achieved.

The sentence or context method

The influence of Gestalt psychology upon the teaching of reading was by no means limited to the look/say approach. There were many who considered the 'whole' to be not the word but rather the sentence, for the sentence expressed a complete idea. The growth of this method though it found psychological support in the Gestalt School, was not an innovation of it. Towards the end of the nineteenth century A. B. Farnham, an American, had advocated the method. Its growth in popularity was due to the work of John Dewey and Decroly and it matured side by side with the project approach to learning.

In its use by Decroly it was merely a starting point for young children, it being considered a legitimate way of building up a basic vocabulary from sentences supplied by the children and therefore using to the full their experience and interests. At a later stage Decroly advocated building upon this basic vocabulary by word-whole and phonic methods. In 1911 Gill produced some research evidence to support this approach.

Decroly's influence upon the English nursery and infant schools was quite marked and it is no doubt from a reflection of Decroly's methods that J. H. Jagger, a London Inspector of Schools, drew the experience for his book *The Sentence Method of Teaching Reading*, first published in 1929. The book is an explanation of the way in which the sentence method had matured in London schools under his influence.

Jagger has a twofold thesis. In his opinion thought takes place only in sentences and the essential part of any reading is the communication which exists between the author and the reader. He sets out the method as starting from discussion of a picture with the children. The children compose their own sentences and selected ones are written beneath the picture. When a sentence can be read fluently with the picture present, the child is directed to match it with an identical sentence and then read it without the picture as a guide. When a number of sentences are well established the child can then be called upon to recognize individual words from them. At a later stage, books are introduced and the child is expected to solve new words by reference to their context.

Since the publication of Jagger's book there has been a steady growth in the use of the Sentence Method, particularly by those teachers who prefer a completely indirect approach to the teaching of reading. Most teachers of young children would agree that the method is included in their approach and some few would consider it worthy of exclusive use. Many reading schemes have been built around the Sentence Method in recent years, e.g. *Pilot Reading Scheme*, *John and Mary Readers* and *Adventures in Reading*.

There are undoubtedly many admirable qualities in this method and these stem mainly from the fact that the approach is a child-centred one. The child provides his own reading matter out of his personal experience for he will only be expected to read sentences he himself has composed during the early stages of reading growth. This ensures that reading will be a meaningful activity within the child's own language ability and not an activity artificially controlled by the author of a reading scheme.

The interest factor is here, as also is the ability to cater for the individual development of children. Why then is this not a complete method? The reason lies in Jagger's refusal to allow the teacher to introduce any method of word building. He asserts that the child will develop his own word building techniques when he feels the necessity for such aids. It must be faced however that Jagger really considered context a sufficient key to unlock the unknown word. This approach to word recognition is, at best, intelligent guesswork and at worst sheer invention. However much we would like to think of reading as thinking inspired by communication through the printed word, we must acknowledge that children can only achieve fluency and confidence in reading if they have some facility in word building. Further, any method in which the child provides his own material brings its own difficulties. The teacher will be heavily taxed if she is to ensure a regular growth pattern in the child's attainment, for the vocabulary will lack control and the repetition rate necessary for memorization will be difficult to achieve.

The Sentence Method must again cause us to look carefully at the reading material which we place before a child. We must ask whether the content is suitable for the child's language facility and his interests. It also demands that the child sees his reading instruction as vital and enjoyable and not merely a set of totally unrelated, uninspired exercises.

Phonic methods
The alphabetic method
Despite the pleas of Comenius for a whole word approach, the most widely used method of teaching reading during the eighteenth century appears to have been the Alphabetic Method. John Wesley, we are told, made remarkable progress in reading, being taught exclusively by this method using a Horn Book and the Bible as his texts. The method was really very simple in its application. The child was taught to recognize the letters and relate the alphabetic name to each. As each new word was met the child read out the alphabetical names of each letter in turn and then said the word itself. It was thought that by working in this way the child would look so carefully at the print that he would not only learn to read but also to spell.

It is hard to see what value the reciting of the alphabetical names had in relation to the resultant word—the whole process would seem to be a hindrance rather than a help to reading progress. Certainly it gave extensive practice in letter recognition and left to right orientation but of necessity it hindered fluency without really giving any aid to the child in unlocking the unknown word. It is doubtful as to whether the child did learn to spell simultaneously as he learned to read, for any spelling improvement resulting from this method would have to come from a knowledge of the complete word.

Strangely, there have recently been a number of revivals of this type of approach. In America there is a tendency to introduce the children to both alphabetical names and letter sounds together in the following manner: 'This is the letter "ay"; it makes the sound "a" as in "apple".' Gattegno in his scheme *Words in Colour* uses another version: 'This is the "white one", it says "a".' The former method may be confusing to the young or dull child for he is being called upon to make two sound responses to the same stimulus, whereas the latter demands a sound response to a mixed stimulus of colour and shape.

The Alphabetic method did not continue without criticism and many felt that if an analytic method was the correct approach then the language should be written in an entirely regular form. Thus experiments began on the one hand in the areas of spelling reform and on the other hand into diacritical systems. Pitman produced the framework of the Initial Teaching Alphabet in 1844 and Richard and Maria Edgeworth set forth a diacritical system as early as 1798.

Diacritical marks

The Edgeworths' diacritical system involved 73 different symbols compared with the 44 symbols found necessary in the Initial Teaching Alphabet and the 41 colours of Gattegno's scheme. This is obviously quite a forbidding prospect for the teaching situation even if it does result in regularity, for teachers know only too well the difficulties of teaching our existing 26 letters to many of our children.

One must admit that all reading includes a certain amount of decoding but here the decoding seems to have become the major activity, nor would it seem to give the child any skill which he could transfer to normal print. This system and others like it invented since that time have never as yet claimed wide support, yet occasionally one finds simplifications of this approach in classrooms today though these are usually limited to the marking of the differing sound values of vowels during the early stages of reading.

The seeds of the phonic approach to the teaching of reading were sown quite early and their influence grew steadily over the years whilst the number who favoured spelling reform failed to gain any wide support.

38

In America the *McGuffey Readers,* which in the early stages were probably used in conjunction with alphabetical approaches but were soon allied to a thoroughgoing phonic technique, were first published in 1820 and remained the most popular readers in American schools until the second decade of the twentieth century. In Britain the phonic method gradually became more refined. As early as 1857 an anonymous author produced the book *Reading Without Tears,* which outlines a fairly scientific phonic approach starting with extensive practice on individual letter sounds followed by joining vowel and consonant. Under this method the child spent many wearisome hours before he ever read a complete word.

Nellie Dale
Though many have credited Nellie Dale with the invention of the phonic method it is obvious that she was able to draw on a wealth of experience in this field. She did, however, bring two new ideas to the teaching of phonics together with a careful analysis of the introduction of sounds judged by their complexity in her book published in 1899.

Nellie Dale's first innovation was her insistence upon ear, hand and eye training. Her children listened to stories, discussed pictures and were encouraged to converse. She also devised simple games and exercises so that children were able to pick out letter sound values wherever they might occur in a given word. Nellie Dale had in fact hit upon a truth which is now expressed in the term 'phonic readiness', and it is obvious to us today that no child would be expected to use a phonic technique before he was capable of appreciating the sound values which make up a word.

Miss Dale also introduced colour as an early aid to the recognition of the sound value of letters and her early reading material made use of these colours. Only four colours were used, as follows:

black print for voiced consonants   red print for vowels
blue print for unvoiced consonants   yellow print for silent letters

These colours were introduced one at a time to the children with appropriate aids to memory, e.g. 'red for vowels for these are important people'. White of course had to be used for voiced consonants when the blackboard was employed as a means of instruction.

This method undoubtedly reflects a teacher who had great enthusiasm, which seems to have remained with her until her death in March 1967, and probably achieved tremendous success. However, the approach is not without limitations. Many children must have found the long preparatory training period irksome and tedious and no doubt many would have learned to read words much earlier had they been exposed to the printed symbol with the sounds he was studying. This represents a confusion between the two states, 'reading readiness' and 'phonic readiness'. For some children these do perhaps go hand in hand but this is certainly not the case for all children.

The use of colour has since been extended by both Moxon (1962) and Gattegno (1962) and possibly has some validity in the early stages of reading. However, though it may help with sound and visual recognition of individual symbols it probably interferes with fluency and good habits of visual discrimination for it is a well known fact that some colours stand out far more than others. Thus with several colours in a word the child might leave all his thorough training behind him and simply guess from whatever feature first caught his eye.

A Ministry pamphlet published in 1933 talks of the Sentence Method as being a new innovation with rather more to commend it than the 'old Look and Say method'. (Infant and Nursery Schools). Nevertheless, it is true to say that the Look/Say method though it grew in prominence during the 1920s, certainly proved no more than a minor rival to the phonic approach. It was during the 1930s and 1940s that the phonic method became relegated to second favourite and indeed disappeared in many infant schools.

There has long been a war between whole word and phonic methods and research continues even today to give very conflicting reports of the validity of each. The answer may well be that this conflict is based on the fact that there is no 'royal road' to reading but rather that the individual child has his own personal way of approaching the task and despite our teaching method learns only in relation to his own peculiar abilities, skills and interests.

In order therefore to be the efficient counsellor of all our children we must be familiar with all approaches and learn how to judge which particular emphasis is best suited to our children as they reach each new stage of reading maturity.

Further reading
DIACK, H. (1965) *In Spite of the Alphabet* Chatto and Windus
DIACK, H. (1960) *Reading and the Psychology of Perception* Peter Skinner

FRIES, C. C. (1962) *Linguistics and Reading* Holt, Rinehart and Winston

MATHEWS, M. M. (1966) *Teaching to Read* University of Chicago Press

MORRIS, R. (1962) *Success and Failure in Learning to Read* Oldbourne

SMITH, N. B. (1965) *American Reading Instruction* IRA

CHAPTER 3

The abilities and skills involved in the process of learning to read

Learning to read is a complex cognitive task demanding a high level of integration and maturity of a wide variety of abilities and skills. It is extremely difficult for the adult to analyse what he is actually doing when he reads for the process has become so automatic and speedy; nor can the adult remember what steps he took and what difficulties he experienced when he first learned to read. Further, the adult, much less the child, cannot give an account of the intricate system of sensations and perceptions which appear to take place during his own reading activity. A good deal of research evidence and observation is available to guide our thinking but there are many questions which, as yet, remain unanswered.

The manner in which reading takes place will vary according to the type of material being read and the purpose for which it is being read. The material and the purpose, therefore, suggest certain approaches to the individual reading task which will be more economical and efficient than others.

The reader must achieve virtually simultaneous processing of three broad areas, namely, an appreciation of the ideas or information expressed, the interpretation of the sentence patterns expressing such ideas or information and the recognition of the words within the sentences. When any of these three areas of activity are absent only part of the reading process is taking place. Thus a child who is asked to work for long periods with words isolated from a meaningful text may be hindered in gaining adequate comprehension in his reading at a later date. From the beginning of reading the child should be provided with materials which are meaningful so that he may acquire the habit of using all the clues available to extract and consider the content expressed.

How is a word recognized?

The recognition of words has often been examined in isolation from meaningful context. As a result there has been a concentration upon the ability of the young child to recognize small complex letter shapes, the size of the fixation span and ability to analyse and synthesize the visual and sound components of a word. The child can, and should, employ his knowledge gained from oral language of the probabilities of certain words or types of words occurring and his understanding of the idea being expressed. Goodman (1970) has termed reading 'a psycholinguistic guessing game'. Certainly the recognition of isolated words is partially a guessing game. Recognition of an unknown word in context is more a problem-solving activity, for the reader has at his disposal a range of strategies which he can use checking each possibility until the word is discovered which satisfies all the constraints of the situation.

Using context

Durrell (1956) states 'without attention to meaning, reading becomes word-calling; without a background of phonics reading becomes a guessing game. With phonics alone, however, reading becomes nonsense syllable analysis.' The child should begin his attack on the recognition of an unknown word by checking the idea being expressed in the sentence and seeing what the unknown word means. Young children tend not to use this strategy unless it is pointed out to them. Often they stop as soon as they meet an unknown word. Had they read on to the end of the sentence a more complete impression of the meaning would have been gained. In the early stages of reading, context clues can very often be extracted from the illustrations in very much the same way. The use of context alone is, of course, an inadequate approach to word recognition, for usually there will be more than one word which has the required meaning. As Durrell suggests context needs balancing with other strategies. Phonic analysis is one possibility but there are a number of others.

Using sentence structure

The young child attains considerable mastery of language, in its spoken form, before he begins to read. Increasingly teachers have realized the importance of this knowledge of the spoken language and the ways in which it can be used to make the early stages of reading more meaningful to the child.

Contrary to popular supposition the 5-year-old has considerable knowledge of English grammar. For example, children working through cloze procedure passages usually choose the appropriate part of speech even when the actual word selected is incorrect. Children seem, therefore, to have a 'feeling' for language; they know what type of word seems to be appropriate on the basis of the store of probabilities which they have already mastered in spoken language. This expands from such simple beginnings as the most likely word to follow 'it' is 'is'. One could however build a sentence on the basis of such probabilities which would be nonsensical, therefore the child must learn to use this strategy along with his use of context.

Using clues within the word

Clues to the recognition of a single word can be gained in the following ways:

1 The general pattern of the word—particularly if it is a short word.
2 The length of the word.
3 The initial letter of the word.
4 The final letter of the word.
5 Distinctive letter groups e.g. 'oo' in 'look' or 'ttl' in 'little'.
6 Phonic analysis/synthesis.

To use these six strategies the reader must employ visual and aural skills, memory, and then check his word against the context in which it is found. In order to use such clues efficiently the young child must develop his linguistic skills and visual and auditory perception and discrimination.

The eye traverses the line in a series of movements and pauses. The eye does not receive a clear image whilst it is moving but when it stops a small area of the page can be seen clearly and a further amount of print will be seen in a more hazy fashion. The pause in which this recognition takes place is termed a fixation and the area of the page which is clearly perceived is referred to as the fixation span. The size of the fixation span varies according to the difficulty of the material being read, as well as the maturity and efficiency of the reader. The young child can probably see only three or four letters in the central area of his fixation span and therefore will often need to make more than one fixation in order to perceive a complete word. This means of course that in a whole word approach or a phonic approach considerable development of short term memory is necessary to see a word as a pattern, or hold the sequence of letters in mind whilst associating a sound value with them. The young child tends to look back frequently in order to remind himself of the beginning of a word and, if he is to read efficiently, these regressive eye movements must be eradicated and his ability to use the peripheral areas of his fixation span increased.

Schonell (1942) suggests that 'the first obvious factor in the recognition of a word is its total pattern'. He qualifies this by suggesting that pattern includes response to words in terms of clues given by length, projecting letters and known groups of letters. Obviously all these strategies used alone would be hazardous and inaccurate.

There is a good deal of conflicting evidence on which type of word is most easily recognizable. Bowden (1911) suggested that words of similar length were the most easily confused whereas Rickard (1935) suggested that the shorter the word the less likely it was to be confused with other words of similar shape or spelling pattern. Davidson (1931) working with children of 3 to 6 years but of mental age 4 years found errors occurred as follows:

Words confused because of similar shape	16 per cent
Words confused with others having same initial letter	18 per cent
Words confused with others having same final letter	10 per cent
Words confused with others having same oddly shaped letter (k, v, w)	7 per cent

Wiley (1928) found that the two chief causes of errors occurring at the rate of 19 per cent were similar endings and beginnings of words, and Wilson and Flemming (1938) studying 6- to 7-year-old children found a tendency to confuse words which had the same intial letter.

That such errors occur is commonplace knowledge to any teacher of young children. Length certainly plays a part in recognition, but only a helpful part when the difference in length between two words is very obvious. Thus the word 'aeroplane' is easily recognized by the majority of children in one of the early books of the *Janet and John* series because it is twice as long as any other word in the book. However, children do not easily distinguish this word among a group of words of similar length, especially if all the words begin with 'a'. I have found that the substitution of any of the following words—acrobatics, anything, applaud, apollonius and apologize, brought the response 'aeroplane' on almost every occasion when presented in the original text to children who were currently reading this book. This may, of course, be very relative to the manner of teaching employed and the subterfuge which was used. Diack (1960) also reached the conclusion that length was a factor, for 'car' and 'caravan' were more easily distinguished than 'caravan' and 'navacar'. When, however, two words such as 'wet' and 'went' or 'play' and 'picture' are confused the difference in length has not been noted by the child. Here the child has seen some letters in certain positions and then responded with the word of which he has most experience, probably from his current reader. It is fairly obvious in fact that a child often responds to a word on the most slender of evidence. Gates and Boeker (1923) quote the example of the dot over the 'i' in pig and Diack (1960) refers to the refusal of a child to match two writings of the word pig because in one the curve of the 'p' did not quite meet the vertical stroke. It seems fairly certain, therefore, that although the young child is capable of making very fine discriminations in a small area, this ability is by no means transferred to the whole of reading.

There is some evidence that children are able to recognize and will derive help from some contact with letter forms. Gesell and Ilg (1946) concluded that letter identification had begun at 4 years and that at 5½ years (these were American children and therefore may not have been to any type of school) most children were fairly familiar with letters. As Diack (1960) has pointed out most of our children see and often work from alphabet books before they come to school so it would be foolish to pretend that we can totally ignore that words are composed of letters. Wilson and Flemming (1938), Gates (1939) and Kopel (1942) all found that good reading achievement and the ability to recognize letters went hand in hand among young children. Nevertheless, M. D. Vernon (1957) sums up the most common point of view today by suggesting that the recognition of individual letters should not be taught until the child has gained a reasonable sight vocabulary of whole words. In support of this contention, those who advocate whole word methods assert that letters are meaningless and often difficult to distinguish from each other. We have already seen that children so far as can be ascertained seem to make considerable use of individual letters, particularly those at the beginnings and ends of words, in order to recognize a word. Again the early stages of reading are accompanied by writing and no child or adult can write without giving attention to individual letters. While one would certainly not underestimate the difficulties involved in letter recognition, the evidence available seems to point to the conclusion that it cannot but be helpful to make the child aware, in some way, that words are composed of letters from the very beginning of instruction.

Diack (1960) has also challenged the suggestion that letters are meaningless. Certainly they have no meaning in the sense that a word or a sentence can have meaning; they cannot convey an idea. However, they have a speech meaning in that they convey instructions upon which the vocal chords react to bring about the enunciation of a certain sound. This is not only important for the child when reading aloud but is an essential stage in word recognition for some type of inner speech is employed by all of us when reading silently in order to relate the word to its context.

It is probably true to say that the child will not remember any word met in print unless that word is linked with a sound value which has meaning within the child's speech experience. McDade (1938) and Duncan (1940) have both suggested that the elimination of sound value in reading would lead to a far greater attainment in reading for meaning. The difficulties experienced in teaching the deaf to read are, however, ample evidence that such an approach would make learning to read more difficult and normal children would probably find it impossible to divorce their spoken language from the reading situation. It would appear, therefore, that there must be a marriage of the visual stimulus with sound before a word can be recognized. It would seem, therefore, that as well as visual clues to word recognition there must also be those of sound and meaning.

The child must be able to link sound to the printed word, but is it necessary to his progress and is he able at such an immature age to make use of letter sounds? If it is true that children gain visual clues to words from individual letters and groups of letters, then the addition of a sound value is going to make his recognition so much more accurate.

The growth of ability to recognize words with accuracy is dependent upon the child realizing the essential order of letters within a word. This realization will only come when the visual stimulus and the sound value of letters and letter groups are equated. This does not in fact mean that a young child can only learn a word by blending its constituent letters. Indeed few children can do this without training for in the earliest stages 'c-a-t' when heard by the child does not bring forth the word 'cat' for he cannot appreciate the mental gymnastics involved in the necessary blending process. Many authorities, e.g. Dolch (1948) have maintained that the ability

47

to blend the letter sounds which make up a word is closely allied to mental age, and whilst there is some truth in this, I would suggest that this skill is also closely related to the type and quality of instruction given to the child. Certainly my own experience does not agree with the statements of Schonell and Dolch that a mental age of 7 years is essential to this activity. Nevertheless there is obvious value to word recognition in any child knowing the most common letter sounds from the very beginning of formal instruction, for these will add to his ability to recognize words and provide a wealth of experience upon which to draw when he is mature enough to use the knowledge within the confines of a phonic approach to reading with its dependence upon the blending of letter sounds. Three possible influences upon the ability to recognize individual words which seem to have achieved scant attention by research are their familiarity, their emotional or situational appeal and lastly the child's increasing knowledge of the probability of certain spelling patterns following a given letter or sequence of letters.

The familiarity of words in the spoken vocabulary of children has gained some attention and the writers of reading material for young children have increasingly considered such studies as Edwards and Gibbon (1964), Burroughs (1957) and Reid (1970). In writing material for publication it is obvious that attention must be paid to words which are known by the majority of children. Familiarity, however, is a very individual matter as Vernon (1948) has indicated. Therefore the only answer to this problem is to make use of the individual child's own language as much as possible through a language experience approach. It will also be necessary to try and ensure that in early readers the child is familiar with the words used or he will be severely limited in his ability to use the various strategies for dealing with words he does not readily recognize in print.

Emotional and situational appeal are again largely individual, but published materials could make very much more use of words which have become commonplace e.g. 'television' and 'space capsule'. The use of word recognition tests can be severely affected by such words. For example the word 'enigma', normally one of the words least often read correctly, was responded to correctly by 38 out of a class of 39 9-year-old children in the last week of a term when in the first week they had listened to and discussed the Enigma Variations. Another example from the same test (Schonell GWRT) has been the rise and fall in the number of correct responses to the word

48

'adamant' with the presentation of a television series *Adam Adamant* a few years ago.

As the child's reading experience grows his familiarity with the spelling patterns of the language will increase. If full advantage is taken of this situation the child should begin to read with an expectancy of what is coming next. We have seen this already from the point of view of the probability of certain words occurring together. Similarly the child can look at the individual word and check its spelling against his knowledge of likely pattern and most frequent variations e.g. 'th' is most likely to be followed by the letter 'e'.

In conclusion, the child should be helped to approach word recognition from all the angles reviewed in the previous pages. He must have all these strategies available and learn to employ them together—not in isolation. It will help the child if the teacher suggests some order in which to apply the strategies, beginning with those which emphasize meaning and using spelling patterns or phonics as a mechanical aid to check the word which has been selected to complete the meaning expressed in the sentence.

The abilities involved in the process of learning to read

We have seen that word recognition is not merely a mechanical process but is closely related to the higher processes of language development and thought. It is easily seen therefore that such a complex activity is going to draw on a wide variety of powers within the child. We must now consider the abilities and skills that are involved in learning to read and we will do so under the following general headings.

1. Intelligence
2. Language facility
3. Visual abilities
4. Auditory abilities
5. Physical factors
6. Environmental influences
7. Emotional factors

1. *Intelligence*

Most people would agree that there is present in every individual an ability which enters into all tasks. The nature of this ability and how far we can estimate its extent in any individual is very much a matter for controversy. Hebb (1949) has pointed out that it is impossible to know the true extent of this ability for any test we can devise to estimate it will inevitably have to draw its result via activities which will involve environmental and emotional factors.

It will be difficult therefore to estimate how great is the importance of general ability in the process of learning to read. Common sense and experience lead us to the conclusion that, on average at least, children who seem to be poorly endowed with general ability have far more difficulty in mastering the process of learning to read than do those who are well endowed. Thus Schonell (1942) and the Middlesbrough Survey (1953) and Kent Survey (1966) found that retardation in reading was more prevalent in those of below average mental ability than in those who had above average ability. This does not, however, mean that the very poorly endowed child has no hope of being able to read for Wall (1946) and Houghton and Daniels (1966) have shown that reading, sometimes of quite a high level is possible for some children hitherto deemed ineducable.

It would appear that intelligence enters into reading attainment in varying degrees at different age levels. Thus Schonell (1942) quotes the following results:

Age in years	8	9	10	11
Correlation of reading with IQ	0·79	0·58	0·59	0·44

P. E. Vernon (1956) found that among students in teacher training colleges the correlation of reading attainment with intelligence was 0·32 for word recognition, and 0·36 for comprehension. All results show a superior correlation between IQ and comprehension than between IQ and word recognition.

We can see, therefore, that although there would seem to be a relationship between general ability and reading attainment, it is by no means a perfect one. There are other variables present such as visual skills and linguistic development and these more specific abilities apparently increase in importance as reading attainment grows over the years.

There is some evidence from Woodrow (1945) and Bliesmer (1954) that mental age is of greater importance than the intelligence quotient in predicting reading success. In the latter research, groups of children were matched for mental age though their chronological ages were widely separated. Both groups were roughly equivalent in the mechanics of reading but the young bright children were superior to the older dull children in comprehension based on the whole texts.

Mental age can be said to apply to the level of maturation reached by any child at a given moment of time. However, various skills mature at different speeds and different ages and as reading employs a variety of abilities and skills, the maturation level given by mental age will refer to only part of the whole picture. Kirk and Johnson (1951) and Collins (1961) have pointed to this factor very forcibly. Collins has proposed that any comparison of reading attainment to intelligence is pointless and that the only worthwhile measure would in fact be a developmental scale which covers a far wider variety of characteristics within the child over a number of years. Whilst one is very much attracted to the idea that the teacher should be able to know every child in such an intimate fashion one must realize the time and expense which would be involved in keeping such records for all our children. Also our ability to estimate some of the characteristics involved, such as personality traits, is itself far from perfect and would thus detract from the accuracy of the picture as a whole. It would seem, therefore, that mental age or some measure of intelligence might still be used as a guide in assessing a child's reading ability especially if the·child is young. We must not, however, make the mistake of expecting a one to one correspondence between mental age and reading attainment for if we do this we will prevent children who are capable of going beyond this level doing so and probably make school a miserable place for the child who is not capable of raising his reading attainment to his general mental level. We will, of course, overcome this tendency if we make a point of studying our children as far as is possible within the classroom, observing growth over a period of time and also know something of the child's home conditions.

2. *Language facility*
Obviously we cannot expect the young child to read from a book words which are outside his experience. When fluency in reading is attained then the child can use his ability to interpret context in order to enlarge his vocabulary and understanding but until this point is reached his reading material must be constructed from words which are within his own spoken vocabulary.

One of the difficulties of finding the relationship between general ability and reading attainment has been the fact that most ability tests are verbal tests and therefore reading ability and/or spoken vocabulary are being tested as well as general ability. Even supposed non-verbal tests are dependent upon verbal instructions. A number of pieces of research have shown this to be a difficulty. M. D. Vernon (1957) found that 6 out of 8 cases of severe retardation in reading had verbal scores well below their performance scores on the WISC test and also did very poorly on the vocabulary test from the Terman Merrill scale. The author tested a group of 130 children on Raven's Coloured Matrices (a test of non-verbal ability) and the Crichton Vocabulary test. These children were aged 7 to 8 plus years and the group had an average IQ assessed on the two scores of 102. The Crichton Vocabulary test scores correlated to the extent of 0·87 with mechanical reading attainment whereas the score on Raven's correlated at the lower level of 0·62 with mechanical reading attainment.

It is clear, therefore, that good language development is essential to good reading, for a good vocabulary and the ability to use language is basic to the process of learning to read.

Language facility is closely related to general ability on the one hand but on the other is very much open to the effects of environmental influences. In other words its development can be enhanced or retarded by the atmosphere in which the child is placed. Thus the child who commences school having spent his first five years in a home where conversation has been at a high level, where his curiosity and enthusiasms have been stimulated and his questions answered will have a decided advantage in reading over the child who has not been drawn into the household conversation nor had so many experiences to excite his curiosity and use of language. Bernstein (1961) has shown quite clearly that a poor social environment causes a general lowering of the child's potential in academic work. Also the child who has a speech defect is more likely to have difficulty in learning to read than a child who is able to speak fluently as Yedinack (1949) reports.

Dialect variations, particularly among vowel sounds, are considerable and may cause the child difficulty in that when the word is met the child might not associate it with the same word in his own speech, nor in fact, ever get to the stage of knowing what a particular word really is. The Lancashire child will probably find difficulty with the sounds 'ar' and 'oo' whilst the Yorkshire child will possibly be confused by the short vowel 'a'. Similar instances can be repeated for children all over the country. However, it is not so readily appreciated that the consonants upon which we depend so heavily in listening to another's conversation are often slurred so that the child finds it difficult to hear them. Thus Fletcher (1953) found that consonants are often heard incorrectly by children particularly the 'p' and 'th' sounds. The obvious moral here is that the teacher must enunciate her words with great clarity and also know the difficulties that the children have owing to their dialect and possibly to a poor speech background at home.

If it is true that the child is less skilled in hearing speech sounds correctly then it follows logically that his understanding of word meanings will also be affected. Ilg and Ames (1950) came to the conclusion that the most important factor in readiness for reading instruction was the child's language facility, for the relationship between the understanding of words and reading achievement is very high.

A number of researches have taken place into the vocabulary of young children and because of the difficulties involved the results have varied greatly in their estimates of the size of such a vocabulary of any given age. Thus M. E. Smith (1926) estimated that children of 5 to 5½ years could use some 2,072 words, Jagger (1929) suggests 2,554 and Watts (1944) from 2,550 to 3,192. A rather different type of research reported by Vernon (1948) observed the conversation of children and amassed a list of 3,000 words used by children between 4½ and 5½ years of age. The astounding result to come from this research was the tremendous variation from one child to another, for among 200 children only 491 words were used in common by 15 or more children. Thus although children may use quite a large number of words there will be considerable variety concerning which words these are from one child to the next. Consequently the vocabularies of early readers will have to be restricted to a small number of most used words. This variation in vocabulary is also a further argument for making full use of individual work in reading based on the interests and vocabulary of each child.

However, this small core of vocabulary possessed by the majority of children is not quite so limiting as it might appear at first sight for McNally and Murray (1962) have stated that some 300 words make up three-quarters of all the vocabulary of children's books. Further a large number of words employed in readers at this age are nouns and usually these can be introduced by the use of pictures. This use of nouns is in keeping with the speech pattern of young children where nouns are the most used parts of speech to the extent of approximately 20 per cent of the total vocabulary. Indeed nouns, pronouns and verbs probably account for more than 80 per cent of the child's conversational speech during the early stages of school life.

Growth in vocabulary seems to be very swift in these early years and children probably double the size of their vocabularies during the stage of infant school education. Vocabulary is somewhat less of a problem than the very limited range of sentence patterns used by children with linguistic difficulties. If a child is to read independently he must be able to gain meaning from a large variety of sentence constructions. It is probable that from the moment the child commences school, it is this institution that is mainly responsible for his language development. Consequently the teacher must foster speech development and language growth within the classroom if the child is going to make good use of the reading instruction given.

There are two factors which are essential to creating an atmosphere which will stimulate and encourage language growth in children. Firstly the classroom must be an interesting, even exciting, place to be in. Young children have a natural curiosity and if fostered by a good supply of attractive objects and pictures, which are frequently changed, then they will observe and wish to converse. Secondly the teacher must give the children the opportunity to speak freely amongst themselves and also to her. But the teacher must not only provide encouragement and a permissive atmosphere, she must also create an example by the clarity of her enunciation and the interesting situations which will help the child to use his language and his powers of constructive thought so that development is encouraged. Language and thought are very closely related and words act as labels or signposts to the knowledge that has accrued from our past experience. Throughout her work therefore the teacher must see that the observations, activities, projects and centres of interest are used not only to interest or occupy the child but also to enrich his store of words and increase his ability to classify his experience. It is probably true that unless experience becomes verbalized it is soon forgotten but at any rate it has certainly not been used to the maximum of its potential. So often children go on a visit, say to a farm, but because no adult named the animals or the plants and explained the processes observed they come away having had an enjoyable day yet having gained little usable experience. The teacher will find that almost any situation can be used to good effect in gaining language experience. The teacher must also observe the children in order to find which children, through lack of previous experience or emotional difficulties, are not able to respond and will devise appropriate individual activities to help such a child.

3. *Visual abilities*
The importance of visual abilities to the reading process cannot be overestimated. These abilities or skills are fourfold but all of course have a physical relationship with the first.

1. Visual acuity
2. Visual discrimination
3. Left/right orientation
4. Visual memory

A child's ability to read print is obviously closely connected with the quality of his sight. In these days of free medical care and regular school medical inspections, gross defects of visual acuity which remain uncorrected are far less frequent in our schools than was the case a few years ago. Nevertheless the author recently visited an infant school reception class in a rather poor area where no less than 9 of the 41 children in the class were suffering from strabismus (squint). It is obvious therefore, that there is every reason for the teacher to be watchful for any child who shows signs of having visual difficulties. It is well therefore to be acquainted with the more common visual defects.

Strabismus (squint) In serious cases one eye has become so weak that it no longer moves with the other eye. This may cause double vision and in extreme cases may result in the eye becoming useless. In minor cases spectacles and exercises can often correct the imbalance between the eye muscles which cause the complaint and thus normal functioning can be restored. Even quite serious squints can be corrected by a comparatively minor operation.

Myopia (short sight) In all but the most serious cases this condition can be overcome by the use of spectacles. The complaint is due to the refractive power of the lens of the eye being too strong thus focusing the image in front of the retina and producing blurred vision. Many children have this defect in a minor form and the teacher must note whether any of her class habitually hold their books very close to their eyes or who have difficulty in seeing the blackboard, sending such children to have their eyes tested at the earliest possible moment.

Hypermetropia (long sight) This is caused by the lens of the eye having a weak refractive power so that the point of focus is in fact behind the retina. Again this defect is usually compensated for by the use of spectacles.

Astigmatism This defect is caused by uneven curvature of the lens of the eye resulting in distortion of the image e.g. a circle may appear as an elipse. Again this defect can usually be corrected by the use of spectacles. This complaint is brought out much more in such activities as reading where concentrated effort and very small discriminations are required and so the teacher will bear this in mind in the case of children who cannot concentrate on activities involving this type of effort.

The teacher must always beware of assuming that because a child has visited the doctor or optician that everything is now in order. Firstly a complete correction of the defect may not have been possible and secondly the prescription may not have been completely accurate. Lastly children must have a period of reorientation to both the physical and emotional effects of any such correction which means that the teacher must expect a period of readjustment while the child relearns his visual habits.

As far as can be ascertained the child starts life seeing the external world as something of a haze. Gradually out of this haze he observes actual objects and later is able to recognize their relationship to himself. The process can be likened to the experience of travelling in a very fast train where the speed of travel is too great even for the adult to make clear and accurate observations, but as the train slows down accuracy increases. It is obvious therefore that the act of light reflected from the objects round us being focused on the retina,

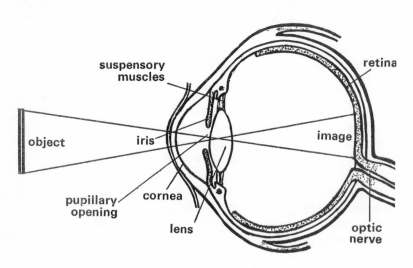

which takes place as long as our eyes remain open, means that we do see these objects. Yet so often we can look at an object and have no knowledge of having seen it. This is due to the fact that any image falling on the retina must be transmitted along the optic nerve to the brain cells and the mind must interpret the sensation which has been received upon the retina. This process is one which we call perception and is a most complex process. The first difficulty is that the lens of the eye inverts and rotates from left to right the image of the external object.

It has been discovered that the mind must train itself by constant exercise in order to allow for the inversion and different orientation of the image received upon the retina. Experiments have taken place where spectacles have been worn which give the retina an image of the object which is not inverted. If worn long enough and the person involved can suffer the accompanying headaches, eventually the perception which now would seem to show objects inverted will allow for the change and set the objects the right way round once again.

If, therefore, the perceptual process is learned in a habitual manner it would seem to follow that the detailed discrimination necessary in learning to read could be aided by skilful training. The young child cannot appreciate small differences such as letter shapes and the order of letters in words, for we have already seen that his perceptual powers gradually increase. We must, therefore, consider this factor when judging whether a child is ready to commence reading or not —if his powers have not matured sufficiently, then we must give him the instruction required to develop them.

Let us examine, however, to what extent the ability to discriminate visually is important to the process of learning to read. Unfortunately the young child cannot describe accurately what he sees or how word recognition takes place. Certainly much of the research concerning word recognition has been done among adults and it may well be that the manner in which a word is recognized by an adult differs from the way it would be recognized by a child. In the absence of such direct evidence research workers have tried to infer what the child is able to see at any given age by requiring the child to copy meaningless figures. This process has its own weaknesses, for meaningless figures are not reading material and the tests also involve the further skill of motor control.

It has been discovered that simple geometrical shapes such as a triangle and circle can be differentiated from each other in matching activities as early as 2 years of age. More complex figures cannot be differentiated until much later and even at the age of 6 years children rarely relate all the constituent parts of a complex shape. The implication here would seem to be that the 5-year-old child is unlikely to see a word as a whole but as a jumble of unrelated details.

However, several investigators have come to the conclusion that the relationship between the power to discriminate among small shapes and reading attainment is very small. Thus Gates (1926) found a correlation of only 0·3 between discriminations of small differences of shape and reading attainment. He came to the conclusion that a minimum level of ability to discriminate among shapes was necessary but this minimum perceptual ability might be quite small. On the other hand many have claimed that training in visual perception has improved reading progress. MacLatchy (1946) stated that practice in the perception of shapes was of help in enabling 7-year-old children to learn to read. These children may of course have been suffering from delayed perceptual development.

Some improvement in our knowledge of the processes involved in perception have recently come from those who have been studying children who have gross difficulties in these spheres. Tansley (1967) stresses the co-ordination of all the senses rather than an over emphasis on any one sense and points to the often neglected sense of touch as being most useful in helping a child to form a concept of shape through the use of language.

Visual perception acts in two ways to aid reading—it is not only necessary to perceive the words but also to be able to interpret pictures for this latter skill is much used in the early stages of reading. Here we must be sure that the pictures are in fact understood by the child for often they give invaluable clues to the recognition of new words.

G. Keir (1951) tells how when designing material for backward readers she found that many such children of secondary school age were unable to name pictures of seemingly common fruits such as a pear. The complexity of the pictures in many of our infant readers is far too great and children often miss the real meaning of the picture even when they can name the items within the picture. In many cases where the picture tells a story rather than the text, the attractive illustration is entirely wasted. Line drawings of the cartoon type seem to be more helpful in this context for they appear to be more readily interpreted by the child. Good use of this type of illustration is made in the *Oxford Colour Books* by Carver and Stowasser.

Left/right orientation

It has been decreed that our language should read from left to right, yet the original decision was an arbitrary one, for some languages are read from right to left and some even from the bottom of the page to the top. The child must learn to move his eyes as smoothly as possible along the line and avoid backward, i.e. right to left, movements. In fact, this movement will not be entirely smooth for it is only when the eye becomes stationary that a clear sensation is received by the receptors within the retina. This period of stopping is termed a 'fixation' and the fewer of these made in any one line of print, the greater will be the fluency of the reader.

It is, of course, extremely difficult for someone trained in our orientation to reverse the process. Yet the very young child appears to be able to recognize pictures equally well when they are rotated and inverted and Newson (1955) discovered that children of 5 years of age are frequently unable to distinguish between a shape and its mirror image. When a child comes to learn to read he must gain proficiency in this skill or he will be at a great disadvantage for a number of our letters are rotations or inversions of other letters e.g. 'b' and 'd' and 'n' and 'u'.

There must, of course, be some form of direction in any written language and there are some advantages in the orientation we have chosen other than those which accrue from extended practice in the medium. The majority of people are right-handed and right-eyed and it is more simple to read and much easier to write when the hand and eye are moving away from the centre of the body to the right. The left-handed and left-eyed child is at a slight disadvantage for he has to work across his body. This causes more difficulty in writing than in reading for it is difficult for the left-handed child to observe the words he is writing.

It is obvious that reading can never be fully efficient until the child has mastered this process of reading from left to right for order and direction are essential to a good standard of word recognition. To the young child who has not yet matured sufficiently to differentiate between an inverted object and one which is the right way up, the letters 'u' and 'n' will appear identical. Again the child who has mastered neither skill will be hopelessly confused by the group of letters 'b', 'd', 'g', 'p' and 'q'.

Such mistakes are very common among children at the infant school stage and fortunately the difficulty does not seem to be of such importance that it prevents reading progress, although of course the eradication of the difficulty must enhance the rate of progress. These errors gradually reduce over the years and even where they persist they are more often a symptom of reading failure than a cause of it. There is a case here for teaching children only the capital letters in the early stages of reading for the differences from letter to letter are greater than among lower case letters. However, this method brings its own difficulties for often children find it difficult to break the habit of using capitals in the middle of words in their written work. One child comes to mind who, even though a fluent reader wrote his name as 'p A u l' at the age of 9 years despite having the error pointed out to him on many occasions.

There is a wealth of evidence to prove that children find letters with reversed orientation such as 'b' and 'd' difficult to distinguish. Frank (1935) found such errors to be very common under the age of 7 years in reading and Hildreth (1932) found that up to 80 per cent of children under 7 years of age made reversals when asked to copy letters. However, Ilg and Ames (1950 and 1951) found that in both reading and writing these errors were disappearing quickly at the age of 7 plus years. M. D. Vernon (1957) reports that only 12 per cent of children between the ages of 7 and 8 years found any difficulty with reversible letters.

Maturation of two skills, one visual and the other auditory, play a part here, for in reading it is not merely a process of distinguishing one letter shape from another, but also of being able to link a sound value with one letter which has a reversed equivalent with a different sound not present on the printed page but possibly confused within the mind.

Ilg and Ames (1950 and 1951) reported that children found more difficulty with the orientation or order of letters within a word than with letter reversals and inversions, especially when complete reversal was possible as in the words 'was' and 'saw'. Word reversals and letter transpositions were still fairly common up to 9 years of age in reading and up to 8 years of age in writing.

It is interesting once again to note that these errors are less frequent in written work, where the child must pay careful attention to each individual letter and its position within the word. In many approaches to teaching reading, children are discouraged from looking at individual letters and thus there is an opening for this type of error to creep in. The importance of the teaching approach must be stressed here for we have seen that children can be taught to appreciate orientation of letters and also to relate these letters to a sound value as early as 3 years of age. Diack (1960) goes so far as to suggest that an over-dependence upon whole word methods results in the child losing his undoubted ability to discriminate between letters and therefore he becomes less efficient in the skill of word recognition. Potter (1946) produced evidence that the tendency to make mistakes due to reversals did not die out naturally but was removed by drawing attention to the letters and their order through such means as phonic training and writing.

We must conclude, therefore, that the maturation process involved in achieving the skill of left/right orientation can in fact be aided by careful training. At the same time it must be acknowledged that failure to master this skill fully at the ages of 5 and 6 years does not prevent a child making progress in reading, but this will not be the maximum possible progress.

Visual memory
In order to read the child is not merely required to perceive words but also to recognize them, i.e. he must be able to relate the new perception to previous perceptual experience. This obviously involves some form of memorization of words and/or letters. Many young children seem to have some difficulty in achieving this and others proceed very slowly to add new words to their vocabulary. Again some pupils appear to remember a word in one lesson and have forgotten it in another. These difficulties probably arise from one of the following causes:
1. An over emphasis on one channel of perception.
2. Insufficient repetition of the word for memorization to take place.
3. Immaturity or defect in long term memory.
4. Poor concepts of shape and orientation.

Research has shown that there can be very wide differences in any one child between his ability to recognize a word he has been shown a few seconds earlier and his ability to recognize a word met say the day previously or perhaps a week earlier.

The authors of the more recent reading schemes have recognized these difficulties and whenever a new word is introduced into the text it is repeated several times during the next few pages. However, none of our reading schemes devised for infants have the amount of repetition necessary to ensure future recognition within the readers alone. It is probably correct that this should be so or the books would become far too boring. To overcome this difficulty workbooks, supplementary readers and apparatus are usually available but the teacher will often find it necessary to devise additional activities to ensure memorization for at least her slower pupils.

Gates (1930) experimenting with children in the early stages of learning to read found the following average figures of repetitions necessary for learning to take place in various ability groups.

IQ	Number of repetitions necessary
120–129	20
110–119	30
90–109	35
80–89	40
70–79	45

Fernald in her work with the kinaesthetic method found the average rate of repetitions necessary to be very much higher than those quoted above but the children concerned, whilst they were older, had been frustrated by failure. It is essential that the above table should be looked upon merely as a guide in designing reading work. The figures are averages and individual children will vary greatly in the amount of repetition they require to memorize any word. Again all words do not require the same amount of repetition —some words may be learned after only being met once or twice because they have a special importance to the child or contain some outstanding characteristic which the child never fails to interpret correctly. Conversely some words will seem to be beyond the capacity of the child to memorize them and when this happens the word is best ignored and left until a later date.

4. *Auditory abilities*

The child's contact with language during his early years comes entirely through the sense of hearing. If for some reason the child's hearing is defective or the speech he hears is slurred and indistinct then his language growth will be delayed and his ability to discriminate between two sounds will be damaged. It is not our purpose here to consider the specialist sphere of the treatment of deaf children but it must be remembered that some children are deaf in certain tonal ranges and others who are prone to catarrh have periods of hearing difficulty.

McDade (1937), Buswell (1922) and Duncan (1940) all suggested that if the sound element could be removed from the reading process the ability to comprehend would be increased. It is to be doubted if this method is possible with normal children and in any case it would bring its own peculiar difficulties. The normal child will always tend to associate the sound of a word with the visual stimulus of the print and though he may be able to read 'silently' there is no doubt that even the experienced adult reader constantly employs sub-vocal speech during reading. It would seem to be an impossibility to conjure up a purely visual image of a word completely divorced from sound. Thus our hearing of language and perception of language sounds is going to aid reading in the following ways.

1. To building up a vocabulary.
2. To act as a further aid to memorization and therefore to the recognition of the printed word.
3. To enable us to hear the constituent sounds of which our words are constructed and use these sounds upon the new words we meet.

Children learn quite early in life, usually between 6 and 12 months, to respond to words spoken to them with a fair degree of understanding but in this they are aided by gestures and intonation and only gradually do they become able to respond to words entirely on the basis of their meaning.

This skill grows through listening and the child's own efforts to reproduce speech. It can be seen, therefore, that speech defects in a child will result in retardation of his own language development and in his ability to appreciate the constituent sounds of the speech of others.

Research has firmly established the fact that at the beginning of school life auditory acuity is weaker than it is in later school years and this is only partially accounted for by the lower ability of these young children to attend. Kennedy (1942), Bennett (1951) and Midgeley (1952) all agree that auditory acuity is only partially developed in children at the infant school stage. However, these researches were based on listening to individual words which is much more difficult than listening to continuous speech even for the adult.

Growth in reading attainment is largely dependent on the ability to attack a word which has not been met before in print. In order to do this the child must understand that:

1. each word has its own sound pattern
2. this sound pattern can be broken down into a series of sounds which are arranged in a definite sequence
3. these sounds correspond to letter shapes or the combination of letter shapes.

This knowledge is essential if any phonic work is to be undertaken and the question arises as to the age in development at which any child is capable of making these distinctions. 1 and 3 above are quite within the capacity of the average 5-year-old child but 2 is much more difficult to fit to a particular age for it depends for its growth upon the maturational process, the individual excellence in auditory perception, good left/right orientation and the training the child is given to bring about such understanding.

The stage at which this takes place, namely the stage of phonic readiness, appears to vary considerably from child to child. The first conclusion we must draw, therefore, is that phonic teaching can never be a matter for class work but must be done individually or within small groups.

Burt (1937) suggested that children might be helped more through the early stages of reading if the teaching method employed was based in whichever major sense modality, visual or auditory, appeared to be the stronger. This sounds most sensible but it must be remembered that reading by all the normal approaches employs both visual and auditory abilities and efficient reading depends upon the two running hand in hand.

In a recent survey the author found that 60 per cent of children in the last term of nursery school seemed not to have reached the level at which the integration of the two senses had developed sufficiently for them to begin reading. The difficulty is that whereas written language is divided up spatially, spoken language to which we ask the child to relate written language, is set out in time. The child must therefore learn to bring these two dimensions together in order to process and extract meaning from written language.

5. *Physical factors*

Any illness or incapacity which results in long absence or inter-mittent attendance at school will usually lead to retardation. Such retardation, however, will be of a general nature rather than a specific nature and, therefore, the teacher will need to keep a very watchful eye on any such children to be found in her class. Fortunately the child experiencing this type of retardation responds quickly to sympathetic guidance. This is not true, however, of the child who is suffering from malnutrition or insufficient rest for here the child has not the energy or power of concentration to make the added effort.

Schonell (1942) felt that a number of physical factors, other than defects of sight and hearing were at least contributory causes of poor reading progress. We have already mentioned the slight disadvantage of the left-handed child in reading and writing in a script which is orientated from left to right. A much more difficult situation occurs when there is mixed handedness and eyedness. The majority of people have established a preference for the right hand and the right eye has become the dominant or leading eye. A further smaller percentage have established the co-ordination of the left hand and left eye. Some people, however, have preferred hands and dominant eyes on opposite sides which makes difficulties with regard to the co-ordination necessary in reading the printed word or in writing. This condition does not necessarily lead to reading failure but would seem to be found in a far higher percentage of poor readers than in the population at large. Schonell gives the following figures from his own investigation.

	Backward Readers	Normal Pupils
	75	75
Right hand and right eye	43	60
Right hand and left eye	40	25
Left hand and left eye	5	4
Left hand and right eye	8	3
Right hand and either eye	3	8
Left hand and either eye	1	0

The basis of crossed laterality appears to be found in the dominance of one hemisphere of the brain over the other. In the case of a right-handed and right-eyed person the dominant hemisphere would be the left portion of the brain. However, many people vary in their preference for a certain hand or eye, and this is particularly so among children, despite the fact that dominance is usually asserted before the age of $3\frac{1}{2}$ years. Burt (1937) suggested that crossed laterality or a lack of dominance was associated with emotional instability and in my own observations, I have noted that children with emotional problems with regard to reading often suffer from mixed handedness and eyedness, but frequently as their reading improves, their emotional life becomes more settled and dominance appears to be established in the use of hand and eyes. On the other hand it would also seem that for some children mixed dominance is an established physical fact without any emotional causation nor is it affected by the normal process of maturation.

The condition of crossed laterality is worthy of exploration in children who have a decided tendency to reversal or inversion in their reading. A higher percentage of children having crossed laterality do make this type of error but by no means all of them. In the Kent survey there appeared to be no relationship at all between handedness and reading ability but crossed laterality does not seem to have been explored.

Clark (1970) did not find any evidence that left-handedness or crossed laterality was a factor in reading difficulty. It seems therefore that though many children do have difficulty with the order of letters within a word and the orientation of letters, this directional confusion cannot be put down to any single cause.

Sex differences
The three surveys conducted by the Ministry of Education into reading standards in 1948, 1952 and 1956 seem to show that reading attainment among boys is slightly superior to that among girls. Most surveys prior to this time and also the 1954 section of the Kent Survey had shown a slight advantage to the girls. This conflicting evidence can only lead us to assume that the Watts-Vernon test employed by the Ministry gives boys a greater opportunity to do well in it than it does the girls. Vice-versa it may also be that some other reading tests favour the girls.

In the follow-up section of the Kent Survey a slight superiority in reading attainment in girls was found but there was a gradual decrease in this superiority over the junior school years. It would seem that this small superiority in attainment is mainly due to better adjustment in school and of superior attitudes to reading among girls than among boys. However, the evidence available clearly demonstrates that sex-difference is not a significant factor in its effect upon the process of learning to read.

6. *Environmental influences*
A number of environmental features which have a bearing upon reading progress have already been mentioned under other headings. We have noted how helpful to language development is a stimulating atmosphere at home where the child can explore and converse with parents who encourage his experiments and curiosity. We have seen also that neglectful homes where children are either poorly fed or not allowed sufficient rest must constantly be at a disadvantage.

In the extensive documentation undertaken in the Kent Survey of

101 poor readers and 98 good readers the following environmental features were discovered. The percentage of poor readers coming from homes with a low socio-economic status was much higher than that for the good readers. A higher percentage of the poorer readers had mothers in full-time employment and their homes had a smaller and less carefully selected sample of books, magazines and newspapers. The poorer readers tended also to come from larger families and/or to receive less encouragement at home. One strange factor which appeared was the fact that 8 poor readers and 9 good readers had lost one parent or lived in broken homes and thus in this research at least, there was no association between the unstable home and poor reading attainment. On the other hand some few of the very good readers had poor home backgrounds judged from the socio-economic standpoint and conversely some of the poor readers came from families which were of a high socio-economic status. Neither the socio-economic status nor even the intelligence of the parents are foolproof instruments for the assessment of the helpfulness and sympathy of the parents towards their children's academic progress. Thus Preston (1939) concluded that there was no relationship between the fitness of parents to bring up children and their socio-economic status or intelligence for she found unsympathetic parents in all classes. It would seem, however, that this lack of sympathetic treatment is due in the higher levels more often to overanxiety rather than neglect.

For the maintenance of good reading progress it would seem necessary to have at least a reasonable background of material provision, but it is probably more important that the child should have a happy relationship with the parents, who in their turn should provide interest, stimulation and sympathy when difficulties arise.

7. Emotional factors

Emotional factors seem to allow a division into two types under the headings of attitudes to reading on the one hand and general personality problems on the other. I have known some children with gross emotional problems and many who have little interest in reading, rarely reading unless directed to do so, whose reading progress has always been satisfactory.

Motivation is, however, of the utmost importance for learning to read is a lengthy process demanding concentration and interest over a number of years before real fluency in the medium is achieved. The importance of the child having an understanding of his work and of the necessity of interest and apparent success are paramount. Success not only breeds success, but also of itself leads to improved attitudes and this probably explains that in the Kent Survey 35 per cent of poor readers liked reading 'a lot' compared with 68 per cent of the good readers in 1956 but in 1957 it was 37 per cent of the poor readers and 87 per cent of the good readers who were able to express this opinion.

Children who come into school with poor attitudes towards reading are probably better having their start upon the reading process delayed in an effort to reorientate the influences which their environment has had upon them. On the other hand children enter our schools having had conveyed to them the opinion that they will quickly learn this important skill and any delay in teaching a child to read must be as small as is possible and be a period full of interest and stimulation or poor attitudes will be reinforced by a feeling of failure.

As has already been expressed the relationship between defects of personality and reading attainment is by no means certain. There is little doubt that many speech defects which are injurious to reading progress have an emotional basis as Madison (1956) has shown. An important point which must be raised in response to Schonell's discovery (1942) that 70 per cent of his backward readers had emotional problems is whether the emotional instability had caused this backwardness or whether the emotional troubles were, in fact, the product of the failure to learn to read. Yet common sense as well as the Schonell and Kent surveys would point to the fact that the child who has emotional problems before entering school is less likely to make normal progress than the child who is well-adjusted.

Further reading

DIACK, H. (1960) *Reading and the Psychology of Perception* Peter Skinner

LEWIS, M. M. (1962) *Language, Thought and Personality in Infancy and Childhood* ULP

LUNZER, E. A. and MORRIS, J. F. (1968) *Development in Learning* Volume 2 *Development in Human Learning* Staples

MORRIS, J. M. (1966) *Standards and Progress in Reading* NFER

SMITH, F. (1971) *Understanding Reading*, Holt, Rinehart and Winston

VERNON, M. D. (1971) *Reading and its Difficulties* CUP

WATTS, A. F. (1944) *The Language and Mental Development of Children* Harrap

CHAPTER 4

Reading readiness

Our assessment of the personality of an acquaintance is frequently coloured by the impression made upon us by that person at our first meeting. In the same way attitudes to and attainment in reading can be deeply affected by the success or failure of the child's first attempts to read a book. At one time it was accepted, at least as a working hypothesis, that when a child was old enough to commence school, he was also equipped to make a start on the reading process. With the growth of interest in child development and the study of human abilities it became evident that all children were not equally equipped to commence a given learning task at any set age. It was recognized that children develop at differing rates, that they are not equally endowed with an innate capacity to learn nor yet are they nurtured in equally stimulating environments. Thus teachers have increasingly made allowances for the different levels of ability and attainment within their classes even though the chronological age range is very small.

It was thus established that the age at which a child could make a successful start on the reading process was a variable, individual matter. Here was born the idea of reading readiness i.e. that point in a child's life when his abilities and skills are sufficiently developed, his personality adequately stable and his interests sufficiently lively for him to make a successful start on his first reading book. The next step of course was to determine when this moment arrived and how we could recognize its arrival. It was at this point that authorities parted company and in the absence of real evidence theories of reading readiness emerged which are now largely unacceptable.

'The child will learn to read when he is ready'

This concept of reading readiness had its roots in developmental psychology which viewed the development of a child as a gradual unfolding of the latent powers within. This view has had comparatively recent support from eminent writers on child development e.g. Olson (1959) and on reading e.g. Hymes (1958). The implication here is that readiness in reading is entirely governed by a process of maturation which will remain unaltered by any effort made by the parent or teacher. Further, these attempts to hasten the onset of readiness can only result in failure and probably create emotional problems within the child. The child is, it would seem, the supreme arbiter in the matter, for if the moment of readiness is governed entirely by maturation then not only are we disallowed from helping the child to learn, we will also be unaware of the arrival of the point of readiness until the child picks up a book and begins to read. Every teacher, however, can call to mind instances of children who have learned to read quickly and efficiently but who until directed by the teacher, had shown little inclination to take the step themselves. This concept of readiness incorporates the 'Micawberlike' philosophy of 'waiting for something to turn up'. One must ask how the child is to be employed in this waiting period, for unless he is gainfully employed he is just as likely to contract emotional problems through seeing others achieve success whilst he falls farther behind, as he is to experience such problems as a result of receiving instruction too early.

   One thing is certain; reading does not suddenly appear. In common with all human attainments it is subject to a process of development wherein each successive stage is built upon that which has gone before. The suggestion that any attempt to teach the skills in the reading process is pointless and can only lead to frustration and failure is a most erroneous idea. We have seen that reading is a complex process drawing together a variety of skills and abilities, some of which begin to develop from the very moment of birth. Bernstein (1961) has shown that a poor language environment has a very limiting effect upon the academic success of children and conversely a good language environment is more likely to create academic success. This conclusion is confirmed in the specific sphere of reading by Morris (1966) who found that the majority of very poor readers came from poor home backgrounds and the majority of very good readers from a better class of home environment. The ability to use and understand speech is basic to the reading process and therefore to help a child to increase his language facility must bring forward the time at which he can successfully read his first book. Again Scottish children seem to be as much as eighteen months in advance of their American peers at the tender age of $6\frac{1}{2}$ years in the sphere of reading according to Taylor (1950). The only substantial difference between the two groups of children studied was the fact that the Scottish children had entered school earlier and thus it can only be concluded that reading readiness can be affected by training and is not solely dependent upon maturation.

'A mental age of $6\frac{1}{2}$ years is necessary before a child can successfully begin formal reading instruction'

Schonell (1949) states that educational research had previously shown that formal reading instruction should not be attempted before a mental age of 6 years had been reached and if such instruction was given before this level of mental development had been reached the child would probably experience failure in the medium. The work of Morphett and Washburne (1931) is that which is most often quoted in this context. They made the suggestion that 'it pays to postpone reading until the child has attained a mental age of six years and six months'. This research was undertaken in America, where children commence school life at least one year later than our children and was based on the observation of 141 children from a rather restricted environment. It can be seen that this piece of research has had a far greater effect than was justified by the design and scope of the original experiment.

In examining the claims for a mental age concept of readiness we must ask, 'Do we all mean the same by the term "formal reading instruction"?' Inglis (1949) points out that in America it is usual to demand that the children can recognize a far higher number of words by sight before reading commences than it is in Britain. This perhaps suggests that reading readiness is achieved when the child is ready for phonic instruction. For our purposes it is perhaps best to consider the onset of formal instruction as the time when the child begins to read the first book in a graded reading scheme.

One must not suppose therefore that this suggested delay in instruction means a complete absence of reading attainment or reading growth before 6 to $6\frac{1}{2}$ years mental age have been reached.

Nevertheless there are numerous difficulties to overcome in putting this concept of readiness into practice. Recently the tools by which we measure mental development have been called into question. Different tests tend to give rather different results especially when used to assess young children. Again mental development does not seem to have an even pattern of growth nor do the various mental activities all develop at the same rate. A child may achieve a score equivalent to that of a 7-year-old child on a non-verbal test, whilst only reaching the 5 year level on a verbal test. From our discussion in Chapter 3 it can be seen that the level of intelligence is only one factor among many which combine to facilitate reading and that some of the other factors involved bear little relationship in their development to the growth of mental age. It would seem therefore that the visual apparatus is sufficiently developed in children by the time they are 18 months old and the linguistic knowledge sufficiently great by the age of 3 years for reading to be commenced on these counts.

There is a wealth of evidence in recent years to suggest that children can learn to read at quite an advanced level long before a mental age of $6\frac{1}{2}$ years has been achieved, yet M. D. Vernon (1967) in reviewing the research into the value of the Initial Teaching Alphabet still suggests that the percentage of reading problems among children would be much reduced if the skill was not taught at all before the age of 7 years. In the same year in which Morphett and Washburne published their research Helen Davidson (1931) reported her work with children of chronological ages 3 to 5 years but all with mental ages assessed as $4\frac{1}{2}$ years. Davidson found that all these children made considerable progress during the four months' experimental period. Hebb (1946) describes how a group of American children who started school at 5 years had a great advantage in reading over a matched group who were not able to commence school until after their 6th birthday. Lynn (1963) tells how his own daughter could recognize 100 words on her 3rd birthday when her mental age was less than 4 years. Durkin (1964), Diack (1960) and Doman (1963) all give many examples of early achievement which could by no means always be attributed to high intelligence nor even to good socio-economic environment.

Whilst acknowledging that maturation and innate capacity will determine to some extent the age at which success can be achieved in reading it must also be stressed that conditions present in the environment or within the actual learning situation play a very significant role. Holmes (1962) found that a low teacher child ratio lowered the age at which a child could benefit from instruction and we are all aware that some teachers teach reading more successfully than others. McManus (1961) found that when parents were helped to prepare their children for reading before they came to school the children were able to progress much more speedily on entry into school. Such evidence has persuaded the United States of America to launch the project 'Headstart' in order to gain an earlier beginning to the educative process for those children whose home background is inadequate.

With the development of new teaching aids and new insight into the child's learning processes we can improve the quality of the learning environment. Moore has found that his invention, the 'talking typewriter', which utters the sound of the letter as it prints the symbol enables children to gain some reading attainment as early as 2 to 3 years of age. The Initial Teaching Alphabet and Words in Colour have both been used with some success among children under 5 years of age, for by simplifying the difficulties involved in the spelling of English they appear to remove one of the stumbling blocks to progress. Downing (1966) reports that in the i t a experiment it appeared that in general children of 4 to $4\frac{3}{4}$ years of age could succeed in i t a but did not appear to be ready for reading when the medium of the traditional alphabet was used.

Lynn (1963) after surveying the literature and research appertaining to reading readiness suggests that the whole concept should be scrapped, for the evidence would seem to suggest that a mental age of $2\frac{1}{2}$ to $3\frac{1}{2}$ years is sufficient for the perception and learning of words without any ill effects, providing that the environment is helpful. Suggestions have been made that the term be dropped in favour of 'pre-reading' or 'early-reading', but to change the name does not change the fact that there is really no division of reading or of reading instruction and no point in time when a child really begins to read. The child is reading in fact from the very first moment he recognizes his mother's face as she bends over his cot and he continues reading as he observes his environment, looks at pictures, recognizes his first letter or word and finally reads a book. To separate the whole process of reading into various stages is to lose sight of the continuing nature of its development and if we do this we may well forget that activities for the growth of language development, visual discrimination and auditory discrimination must be continued when the child has commenced the graded reading scheme if maximum growth is to be achieved. It remains important that we should retain a concept of readiness, but a revised one which keeps before us the knowledge of the individual attributes and progress of our children and also the order, division and nature of skills to be learned. There would seem to be therefore a multiplicity of stages of readiness as the child gradually climbs step after step up the ladder to automatic word recognition, full understanding and appreciation of the printed word. Vygotsky (1962) has suggested that when any learning takes place a new and wider 'zone of potential development' is created. There is still, however, a necessity for further research into the most appropriate steps by which learning to read can most helpfully take place.

Many books concerning the teaching of reading provide a list of skills, abilities and interests which must have matured to a certain degree before the child is ready to read. In these lists will be found items such as the following:

1. The perceptual maturity to recognize the shapes of letters and the varied patterns of the printed word.

2. The ability to recognize the sound units from which spoken words are formed.

3. A good speech vocabulary and an ability to use and understand spoken language.

4. A wide range of experiences.

5. An interest in books and the ability to treat them in a respectful manner.

6. Ability to concentrate.

Such lists are not very helpful to the class teacher and have a danger of prolonging the idea that there can be a distinction between a preparatory stage and 'real' reading. We know that the child must have some maturity in visual and auditory powers of perception, yet we do not know how much maturity is necessary in these areas. Indeed we have already noted the opinion of Gates (1939) that the amount of visual discrimination required in reading may be very small. Again the child should have a good vocabulary and a wide range of experience but we might well ask—how many words and experiences, which words and which experiences?

It would seem that such a list might give us some idea of the activities we need to plan in order to gain growth towards reading and perhaps help us as a series of questions when considering whether a child has reached the stage of being able to work within the limits of a graded reading scheme. Insofar as the above headings are unscientific generalizations they are of little use in helping us to assess the total readiness of the child to proceed to the next stage in learning to read. Most reading readiness tests have been constructed with such divisions of the reading process in mind but their prognostic value with regard to future reading progress has not been very good and their interpretation whether by full score or by profile is a hazardous affair. Infant school teachers in this country have shown little interest in test material for establishing the maturity level of children in the skills involved in the reading process and have preferred to trust to their own powers of observation. All too often however their ability to estimate this level has been reduced to a simple distinction between whether the child is ready for a graded reading scheme or not, with insufficient appreciation of the growth towards this point. What is needed is a graded guide to pinpoint the level of development attained by the individual child and which also suggests activities which will help that individual to take the next step in his own growth pattern. An attempt to provide such a diagnostic scheme will appear in Chapter 14. In conclusion it must be stressed that no one stage is completely distinct from another and therefore it will be found that children will benefit from the continuation of skill training even when they are reading books.

It can be seen from the foregoing discussion that the attention of most studies in reading readiness has centred around the question of when without paying particular attention to what and how. The three questions must be asked together for Gates (1937) and more recently Thackray (1972) have pointed to the fact that readiness is not merely a matter of general maturity or even maturity plus past experience, but must be viewed in terms of what materials the child is to use and how he is expected to use them.

Thus any check list or test used must bear some relation to the learning situation which is to follow. In a perfect state it would be possible to allow for all individual variations in abilities, interests and personality. Schools have not usually the wherewithal to provide for all such contingencies and must therefore look towards the range of possibilities available.

An interesting example, despite its lack of scientific sophistication, is the Mills (1954) *Learning Methods Test*. This was based on the assumption that children would benefit most if early learning of reading took place when instruction was weighted towards one of four approaches—language experience, whole-word, phonic or kinaesthetic. The test was devised on relatively informal lines to discover which of these four methods appeared most appropriate for the individual child.

Restrictions upon teacher time and material provision may make the situation described above an impossibility for the teacher. However whatever the situation the teacher must analyse it and find

75

what abilities and skills need to be developed before the child can successfully master the learning involved. The teacher should know what type of mental operation is involved and the level of thinking required. Some previous learning will be assumed by the new learning the child is to be asked to undertake. It will be necessary to find out what previous learning is required, whether the child has fully mastered it, and in what ways the new learning can be related to the old.

Finally the extent to which the child is motivated to read is paramount. Downing (1971) has suggested that the majority of children are not naturally anxious to learn to read on entry to school around the age of 5 years. Most infant teachers take care in creating an environment and atmosphere where reading can be seen to fulfil a useful purpose and be an enjoyable pursuit.

Further reading

DOWNING, J. A. and THACKRAY, D. V. (1971) *Reading Readiness* ULP
FARR, R. and ANASTASIOW, N. (1969) *Tests of Reading Readiness and Achievement* IRA
GOODACRE, E. J. (1971) *Children and Learning to Read* Routledge and Kegan Paul
GODDARD, N. L. (1962) *Reading in the Modern Infant School* ULP
THACKRAY, D. V. (1972) *Readiness to Read* Chapman

PART TWO

Choosing an approach

CHAPTER 5

Methods and innovations

The most important factors in choosing methods, teaching techniques and materials are the individual needs of the children who are to be taught. Yet, however idealistic he may be in this direction, the teacher is forced in the final analysis to make a selection based on the average needs of the group. This is due not only to the fact that the teacher must be concerned with a class of 30, 40 or even more children, but also to the limiting nature of money for equipment and time available. The teacher is faced with a very wide choice of methods and materials—often the latter are allied to the former, but by no means always so. In this chapter and the two to follow an attempt will be made to consider modern innovations, methods and materials in the hope that teachers will be aided in making their decisions in the light of all available knowledge.

The medium
Attention has already been drawn to the fact that one reason for the difficulties experienced by some children in learning to read is the inconsistent spelling of our language. We have noted how the Edgworths designed a diacritical system in an attempt to overcome the lack of relationship between sound and symbol, how Nellie Dale used colour as an aid to letter sound recognition and also the spelling reform movements. Recently there have been a number of attempts to provide help in the early stages of reading by modifications and aids to increase for the child the relationship of sound and symbol. This movement calls into question the old dictum that nothing should be taught which later must be discarded. We must ask, 'Does learning in a modified medium have a helpful influence upon future learning in traditional orthography?' Ausubel (1963) in suggesting that learning in a given area is more efficient if preceded by a particular kind of other related subject matter also asserts that

there is a great need for further research into this whole question. The answer to this problem must, therefore, remain only partially answered for the moment.

The Initial Teaching Alphabet (ita)

The Initial Teaching Alphabet has been the most publicized innovation concerning reading in recent years but it must be remembered that it is not so much a method of teaching reading but rather a redesigning of the material to be read. Indeed at the beginning of the research into the value of ita teachers using the medium were instructed to use the methods which they had used when teaching reading through the medium of traditional orthography.

The alphabet in its first form was designed in 1837 by Isaac Pitman and this phonetic system was used in American schools after revision by Pitman and Ellis in the 1850s under the title of 'Phonotopy' which simply means printing by sound. Sir James Pitman redesigned this alphabet in the 1950s, and it was introduced as an aid to the early stages of teaching reading under the title of 'The Augmented Roman Alphabet'. This new alphabet became the subject of a wide piece of research under the direction of the Reading Research Unit of London University Institute of Education in 1961. Experimentation with the medium received a setback in 1967 when the work of the Unit had to cease owing to lack of funds.

Pitman attributes our reading failures and the painfully slow progress of many other children to the difficulties inherent in our language. The English language is undoubtedly full of inconsistencies for the same letter or group of letters is pronounced differently in different words whilst the same sound can often be spelt in a variety of ways. J. C. Daniels has estimated that 87 per cent of our words can be analysed phonically but this includes many words which are far from regular from the child's point of view and necessitates the learning of a large number of rules in order to solve them. Pitman estimates that 40 per cent of our words are completely regular, i.e. they can be analysed on the basis of one letter, one sound. Examples of the inconsistency of our language are easy to find, e.g. the sound ōō represented in ita by the symbol 'ⲱ' can be written in 18 different ways as in—truth, rude, do, prove, fruit, cruise, group, troupe, manœuvre, shoe, two, zoo, flew, through, wooed, snooze, rheumatism and true. Again the letter 'a', if one includes its combination with other vowels has at least 18 different sounds. The Initial Teaching Alphabet is not entirely consistent in its sound/

symbol relationship but is probably 95 per cent so and this figure is probably higher if analysis is undertaken among children's literature for the early stages of reading.

A further difficulty is to be found in the variations of type used in the printing of early reading books. Most publishers are now selecting a simpler and clearer form of script and such letters as 'a' and 'g' are thus not the cause for concern which they were a few years ago. This is not the case, however, when one compares our capital and lower case letters which in many instances bear no resemblance to each other. The Initial Teaching Alphabet has no capital letters. Instead majuscules are used and these are simply a slightly larger version of the appropriate lower case letter.

Pitman has stated that experience with the medium will no doubt lead to modification in the alphabet itself. This has already taken place in that the original 43 symbols have been increased to 44 in the printed texts and some teachers are now using a variation of the long 'a' where local dialect causes difficulties. It would, of course, be a simple matter to make the sound/symbol relationship 100 per cent accurate, but this would either greatly increase the number of symbols or reduce the visual relationship to traditional orthography. The former would make for initial difficulties in memorizing the symbols, the other would make transfer to traditional orthography more difficult.

The 44 characters used in printed texts are set out below. It will be apparent that 24 letters from our existing alphabet are retained and 20 new symbols are added, many of the new symbols are designed to present a single representation in print of diphthongs and digraphs.

apple arm angel author bed cat chair doll eel egg finger girl hat

a ɑ æ au b c ꜯh d ꬲ e f g h

tie ink jam kitten lion man nest king toe on book food out oil

ie i j k l m n ŋ œ o ꭢ ꞷ ꝋ oi

pig red bird soap ship treasure tree three mother due up van window

p r ɾ s ʃh 3 t ꬔh ꭇh ue u v w

wheel yellow zoo is

wh y z ʒ

Sir James Pitman claimed that children would learn to read more quickly, ultimately become more proficient and be able to transfer to traditional orthography without difficulty, if the new alphabet were used. The Reading Research Unit set out to test these claims and made its first full report in 1963. This report seemed to show that Pitman's claims were justified for in the controlled experiment far more children in the ita group had begun to read and their average standard of attainment in mechanical reading and speed of reading was significantly higher than that of children in the control groups using traditional orthography. It was also reported that the ita children were in no way inferior in comprehension and spelling ability when they returned to traditional orthography and that their creative writing appeared superior when judged for sentence length and grammatical complexity. The second major research project undertaken by the Reading Research Unit did not show statistically significant gains in accuracy, comprehension and speed for the children using ita as compared with those using traditional orthography although the average scores of the ita children were slightly better. From an experimental point of view it is established that ita has some advantages but a more searching analysis of its use is still required before one could entertain the suggestion that all children should use it. One major step would be the organization of small clinical experiments to examine ita in comparison with other simplified spelling systems.

It would seem that in the very early stages, word recognition is made easier for the child and, therefore, success could be achieved earlier with ita. Again the child's desire to express his thoughts in writing can be more easily satisfied and as a result he will not be prevented from being creative in his work by early unhappy experiences in the realm of written language. This same happy start to reading should also lead to more people finding reading to be a truly enjoyable pursuit. Some of our children may be rescued from failure particularly those whose visual memory appears to be very weak. Lastly some of our children could probably learn to read at an earlier age than is the case at present, for ita has pointed to many fallacies in our concept of reading readiness.

We have still to gain information about a number of matters which are related to this medium. We know little about the way in which the young child perceives a word nor are we certain that the combined symbols such as 'ɕh' and 'ʃh' are seen as single symbols or whether they are recognized as consisting of two symbols. Further some children appear to have difficulty in producing the new ita characters and this detracts from the value of the writing process as a whole and its place as a means of the consolidation of reading progress in particular.

Little has been said about the methods of teaching using ita and it would seem apparent that a new medium might reasonably require a new approach. It is probable that ita has most to offer to the teacher who wishes to employ a language experience approach to reading. Much will no doubt be learned from the experience of teachers in Britain and the USA for up to ten per cent of schools in these two countries now use i t a. I t a has not achieved the success hoped for with a minority of dull children nor in remedial work.

Two other items of administrative concern must be made. There are as yet insufficient books published in the Initial Teaching Alphabet to enable the teacher to provide the same variety of reading experience as is possible when using traditional orthography. Few of the basic schemes have been written with ita in mind and therefore some of its value may well be lost. In our modern society transfer of children from school to school is an increasing problem and thus a use of different media for initial reading may cause individual children great hardship.

In conclusion it must be stressed that ita is a change in the medium —it does not teach itself, good teaching will still be necessary. Again not all our present failures will be saved simply by a change in the medium of reading for their difficulties lie in personality defects or environment rather than in the difficulties inherent in our written language.

Further reading
DOWNING, J. A. (1967) *Evaluating the Initial Teaching Alphabet* Cassell
DOWNING, J. A. (1967) *The ita Symposium* NFER
PITMAN, J. and ST JOHN, J. (1969) *Alphabets and Reading* Pitman
WARBURTON, F. W. and SOUTHGATE, V. (1969) *ita: An Independent Evaluation* Chambers and Murray

Words in colour
A second method of simplifying the medium for the initial stages of learning to read is to identify the sounds of the language by colours yet at the same time keeping the traditional spelling of the language. We have seen an early attempt of rather a different type in the work of Nellie Dale, and Moxon has made use of the method in his remedial reading apparatus.

Gattegno introduced his scheme *Words in Colour* in 1962, his intention being to reduce English to a truly phonetic language without altering the spelling of the words. He has achieved this by analysing the language into its constituent sounds and then indicating the sound whatever its spelling by a colour. In order to achieve this 47 colours are used and these colours are placed on Fidel Charts which list all the differing ways in which the sound is represented in English spelling. The colours are also used on the 21 charts which are used for class or group work and will also be used on the blackboard in the very early stages of the scheme's introduction. The colour system is never used in the books which form part of the scheme but the child will have the Fidel Chart around the room for reference if needed. Indeed the method of approach suggested by Gattegno could be undertaken without the use of colour to simplify the medium in the initial stages. The books which Gattegno has written to be used alongside this approach do not use colour nor are they illustrated. Further interesting features are the complete lack of punctuation and capital letters and the inclusion of nonsense syllables.

Using at first the five vowels only Gattegno intends the children to master, the following three points:

1. Each sound has one corresponding sign and each sign one corresponding sound.

2. The sound is said as many times as it is written.

3. When signs (letters) are linked it represents a shortening of time and pauses are shown by spaces between letters. Thus the child is trained to respond to letters individually and in groups and therefore the seeds of word and sentence reading are sown by exercises such as:

| a | aa | aaa | a | aaaa |
| aeu | iou | aeiu | oeiau | |

The child is required to read material of this sort under an exercise which Gattegno terms dictation but it has much in common with the old form of phonic drill where the child had to suffer a long and laborious series of exercises leading to the mastery of the visual and oral qualities of each letter before he was ever allowed to try out his skill upon a word. Certainly the introductory work in this method contains a lot of drill. Gattegno suggests that the children enjoy it and that reading growth is so rapid that the drill itself never gets in the way of intelligent reading later on. Indeed, the method very quickly gets to the English word for after the introduction of the five vowels the consonants 'p' and 't' are added and the child now joins consonant and vowel.

e.g. ap, pa, ep, pe, op, po, ip, pi, up, pu

likewise, using 't' and by simple amalgamation the child can now read:

at, et, it, ot, ut, pat, put, pet, pit, pot, pap, pup, pep, pip, pop, tap, tup, tip, top, tep, tat, tut, tit, tot, tet

The child is encouraged to form all combinations of the letters and then by virtue of his language experience he separates the words from the nonsense syllables and can take the first step in building sentences and when the next sound 's' is added a good number of sentences can be formed:

e.g. pip pats spot

Gattegno must be congratulated on the scientific excellence of his analysis of the English language and on the way in which he enables the child, whilst using a completely phonic approach, to read and write words and sentences so quickly. However, many teachers have been put off the method by the claims Gattegno makes regarding the speed at which fluency can be achieved by children using this method.

Gattegno's approach has not had the attention from research workers which it would seem to merit. Lee (1967) quotes an experiment in Ayrshire where matched groups of children were observed using the three media ita, *Words in Colour* and traditional orthography. After 6 months of experimentation there was no significant difference in attainment among the groups but after twelve months the average reading ages for the groups were:

Traditional orthography	7·6 months.
Words in Colour	6·4 months.
ita	6·1 months.

Brimer (1967) has conducted a short term experiment to test the effectiveness of a number of media for the extent to which they aid word recognition. Here again *Words in Colour* and ita seem to be less helpful than a number of other media. It might be suggested that both these trials were rather unfair to the media involved, for in *Words in Colour* at least the emphasis should be on written English rather than responding to the printed word.

Further reading
GATTEGNO, C. (1962) *Words in Colour* Educational Explorers

BRIMER, M. A. (1967) in W. D. WALL (Ed) *New Research in Education* NFER

LEE, T. (1967) in A. L. BROWN (Ed) *Reading: Current Research and Practice* Chambers

MURPHY, M. L. (1966) *Creative Writing* Educational Explorers

MURPHY, M. L. (1968) *Douglas Can't Read* Educational Explorers

Colour Story Reading

This approach was introduced after preliminary research into children's ability to use colour as a means of identification. Considerable support was gained for the view that children not only enjoy colour but that they use it more than shape in studying their environment. Jones followed this preliminary research by designing reading materials which were given an extensive trial before publication in an experiment organized by the Reading Research Unit.

The approach is somewhat different from Gattegno's. Three colours and black are used together with three background shapes (square, circle, triangle) in each colour to isolate common sounds which have variable spellings. The letters inside the background shapes are black. Short vowel sounds are coloured blue or green and long single vowels are red. The consonants and some common diphthongs are also split among these three colours so that there is differentiation between hard and soft c and g and between such confusing orientations as d, p, b and n, u. There are some irregularities left so a 'nonconformist' symbol is used. This is a black letter with no background shape. There are in fact few of these and most are fairly regular as for example the 'v' sound in 'of'.

Jones proposes the use of colour only as a starter and its use would largely have disappeared by a reading age of 8 years and would then only be used for the introduction of new words.

The teaching method is based on an audio-visual approach. Nineteen stories which are available in book form or as long playing records are used to impart a knowledge of the sounds of the language and the colour system to be used. Each of the characters in the stories represents a particular sound and the stories appear in summarized form in the three children's readers. In this way the children grow used to the fact that the short vowel 'a' is a green apple and the short 'u' a blue umbrella. These characters undergo amusing adventures which appeal to young children. Colour is used in the children's books and they enjoy using colour in some of their written work.

Ample opportunity is provided for dramatic activity and imaginative writing based on the letter characters.

The extensive use of colour in this form does raise some questions. It has been suggested that there is no transfer problem such as is experienced in simplified alphabets. This is not strictly true since children respond to various colours in different ways and will therefore be drawn to recognize words from differing features which could cause difficulty later on. I have noted a number of children who found the black letters against a coloured background difficult to see and needed help in written work where only the outline of the coloured background was used.

The colour coding system used is basically simple and would therefore seem to commend itself for use in remedial work. Many children are indeed helped in this way but many seem to find the reading material somewhat ridiculous. Remedial teachers wishing to use the scheme will at present have to devise and produce materials more suitable to the interests of the older child.

Further reading
Jones, J. K. (1967) *Colour Story Reading* Nelson

Other uses of colour
Colour is growing in popularity and many schemes have been published or will be in the near future. Bleasdale produced *Reading by Rainbow*, a series of four books based on a traditional phonic approach. A not dissimilar scheme has recently been produced by Thomas Wood.

The *Wordmaster Major* uses colour as a simple means of making print more attractive to the child in reading games of the lotto type.

Moseley (1969) has devised a scheme which he calls English Colour Codes in which vowel sounds are isolated by colour. This is used in a series of tapes and workcards which will be described later (page 99).

Further reading
BLEASDALE, E. and W. (1968) *Reading by Rainbow* Moor Platt Press
HARDIMENT, M., HICKS, J., KREMER, T. (1969) *Wordmaster Major* Macdonald
MOSELEY, D. V. (1970) *English Colour Codes Worksheets and Tapes* National Society for Mentally Handicapped Children

A Linguistic Approach

The third way in which the medium of our language can be modified is to scheme the introduction of words so that only the entirely regular spellings of the sounds of the language are introduced during the early stages. To a certain extent Daniels and Diack follow this plan in their 'Phonic-word' method which we will consider shortly but here we will examine the approach set out by Fries (1962) and based upon ideas previously set out by Bloomfield (1961).

Fries suggests that reading growth should be divided into three stages:

1. *The transfer stage*

The first essential is said to be the learning of high speed response to the visual presentation of the letters. This would be undertaken without letter names, sounds or written work. Letter names are dismissed as totally unimportant, letter sounds as having little value since our language is so irregular and writing, as it is considered a secondary skill, is unimportant at this stage. Thus the child is required to work through numerous recognition exercises starting with the capital letters introduced in strict order with regard to their manner of construction. These exercises are of the matching type, the child being presented with pairs of letters and saying whether they are the same or different.

e.g.
```
I     T
T     T
I     I
T     I
F     T
F     F
E     F
```

When this has been achieved recognition of letters in groups follows:

```
IF      IT
TF      TF
TF      FT   etc

FIT     TIF
FIF     FIE
FEI     FEI   etc
```

Part two of this Transfer Stage is to learn to respond in the same speedy and automatic manner to the spelling patterns of English. Individual letters are never sounded but the whole word is spoken. Words are learned in rotation of their spelling complexity and the contrasts between spelling patterns are pointed out, e.g.

AT — CAT
CAT — RAT
FAT — HAT etc

The teacher will say each new word as it is introduced and make certain that the child has the word within his language experience.

Fries outlines two further stages which do not really concern us here whilst we are considering the initial stages of reading only. However, in fairness to the approach as a whole we will briefly outline their content.

2. *Productive reading*
Fries here stresses the importance of reading with understanding and the portrayal of this understanding by expression and intonation in reading. As reading is a form of communication then this skill must be developed and practised.

3. *Vivid imaginative realization*
When the reading process has become entirely automatic then the child can assimilate new experience not only through knowledge but also through an aesthetic appreciation of the beauty of language and further a realization of the depth of emotions and values as presented by the literary artist.

Fries considers that the Transfer Stage will probably extend over 500 to 1,000 hours of practice for the child. This in itself is a vast amount of time to spend on mere drills and one cannot help but wonder whether this excessive drill, to gain high speed recognition responses to letters and spelling patterns, might well prohibit the child having the emotional drive to achieve the heights of excellence envisaged in the stage of 'Vivid Imaginative Realization'. One might also question the decision to omit letter sounds and written work. Again books based on this approach remind one of the stilted text of the phonic reader of years past.

Wardhaugh (1969) has questioned whether there can be such a thing as a linguistic approach to the teaching of reading and has suggested that the contribution of the linguistic scientist is to help us understand the nature of the written code we endeavour to teach.

Certainly linguistic scientists are no more unanimous concerning the nature of the approach to beginning reading than any group of infant school teachers are likely to be.

Lefevre (1964) for example takes an almost opposite point of view to that of Fries reviewed above, and insists that all attention to spelling patterns should come after the words have been experienced in a meaningful context. He suggests that the smallest unit of meaningful language is the sentence.

The *Breakthrough to Literacy* materials are an attempt to bridge the gap between these two approaches. They begin by encouraging the child to produce his own language and then analyse the spelling patterns of the words used and with the teacher's help make generalizations concerning the sound/symbol structure of words from them.

The central materials are found in the Sentence Maker and the Word Maker. The former consists of a folder containing a number of more common words selected on the basis of the frequency with which they are used and their representation of the more common spelling patterns of English. The child uses these words to build sentences which he has composed and the teacher adds other words as the child needs to use them. The word folder is an alphabetically arranged wallet of letters to provide material for word building.

Breakthrough to Literacy is not a scheme in the traditional sense. Its success depends on the teacher's ability to create a need for the child to record language in a written form and to enable the child to build a knowledge of the spelling patterns of the language on the basis of the words provided by the child.

Further reading
FRIES, C. C. (1962) *Linguistics and Reading* Holt, Rinehart and Winston
LEFEVRE, C. (1964) *Linguistics and the Teaching of Reading* McGraw-Hill
MACKAY, D. *et al* (1970) *Breakthrough to Literacy: Teacher's Manual* Longmans

Key words
One of the major difficulties in the production of reading matter for children is the choice of words used and the order in which to introduce them. This is doubly difficult when the author is at pains (a) to produce literature which is meaningful and interesting and (b) to secure growth in attainment for the child. Analyses of litera-

ture notably by Dolch in the USA and Murray and McNally in this country have revealed some amazing facts. The latter claim for example, that the following twelve words form one-quarter of all words read and that some 300 words make up three-quarters of all our literature.

a   and   he   I   in   is   it   of   that   the   to   was

It was but a small step, therefore, to suggest that if these words were taught well in the early stages the child would be greatly helped to interpret those words used less frequently by the context in which they stood and the width of literature available to the child could be greatly increased.

There is little doubt that the work of these men has been most helpful but neither of them would claim that they have produced an all embracing approach to teaching reading but rather an aid to the teacher in recognizing the relative importance of words in consideration of their frequency. Their work has certainly influenced the authors of most recent reading books. Murray himself has produced the *Key Words Reading Scheme* around his research and Tansley and Nicholls' *Racing to Read Scheme* is based in an analysis of children's written work. Most companies which provide reading apparatus have devised games to encourage memorization of these words e.g. Philip and Tacey—Basic Word Lotto.

Although there is here a definite aid to us in our teaching, it is of limited value. Firstly, many of these most used words are neither nouns, verbs nor adjectives and consequently are difficult to teach by normal look/say approaches. Secondly, many are also irregular with regard to spelling and, therefore, cannot be taught in a phonic manner. Again when a child reads a sentence, context methods of discovering an unknown word are less likely to be successful if the nouns and verb are the words which the child does not recognize. We should take note, however, that these words are important by nature of their frequency, and endeavour to gain for our children, early memorization of them.

Further reading
Dolch, E. W. (1951) *Psychology and the Teaching of Reading* Garrard Press
Edwards, R. P. A. and Gibbon V. (1964) *Words Your Children Use* Burke

McNALLY, J. and MURRAY W. (1962) *Key Words to Literacy* School-master Publishing Company

The phonic word method

The designers of this approach, Daniels and Diack were the leaders in this country of a new movement which has been termed the 'Phonic Revolt'. Daniels and Diack believed that the whole word and sentence methods were psychologically unsound approaches to the teaching of reading and were at least partially responsible for many of our children failing to master the reading process. In fact, all existing methods of teaching were submitted to severe criticism.

The traditional phonic approach was criticized because the sounding of individual letters did not give the child the ability to blend them into the original word.

e.g. 'ke–a–te' does not make 'cat' nor does 'be–uh–te' make 'but' but rather 'butter'

The suggestion here is that the relationship is not one of pure sound but rather an abstract relationship which grows only with long experience and maturity. Secondly, the vocabularies of existing phonic reading books were unrealistic, dull and limiting and progress was maintained by uninspiring drill and repetition. Thirdly, the method employed of sounding out a word had pitfalls for a letter is frequently modified in sound by a later letter, e.g. 'rag' and 'rage'. Lastly, the letter sounds on their own are not, strictly speaking, language, though they are part of language and have meaning in that they carry instructions for the production of sound.

Whole words methods were attacked because they ignored the fact that letters have a definite part to play in word recognition and that it is virtually impossible for a child to recognize a word by its shape. It was stressed that such methods encouraged guesswork and careless reading habits and the texts used were, in many cases, less meaningful than the old phonic books, due to their high word repetition rate and the selection of vocabulary on the basis of the widely differing shapes of words.

Daniels and Diack established three principles upon which they felt early reading instruction should be based:

1. The materials should be well illustrated 'active' materials.
2. They should sustain the interest of the children.
3. They should lead the children, step by step, but as rapidly as

possible, to an understanding that letters in words stand for sounds in a certain order and should begin by teaching the child the most common sound-values of the letters.

They set out to devise an approach which they later termed the phonic word method and this method can perhaps be viewed as having drawn from existing look/say and phonic method those facets which seem to be most worthwhile. The child is introduced to a number of pictures which illustrate 3-letter words e.g. 'top', 'tap', 'tin', and 'tub', and his attention is drawn to the beginning sound of the word, in this case the letter 't'. The letter sound is, therefore, introduced as an integral part of the word itself. The child will proceed to meet this letter in various positions in other words and will be able to fill in missing letters in the words he has learned because of the joint visual and aural knowledge he has gained. The children will be asked to give other words which begin or end with sounds that they are learning, but no effort would be made at this stage to introduce more complex spelling-patterns such as might be suggested, e.g. 'tree' or 'table' into the reading matter. A careful analysis of the spelling patterns of our sounds and words has been produced so that reading vocabulary growth is largely governed by the phonic complexity of the words. The importance of comprehension is not neglected and from the earliest stages the child is asked to complete exercises which can only be done correctly if the child pays attention to the meaning of the sentences he is reading. Daniels and Diack realized that the irregularity of our language militates against a thoroughgoing phonic approach and consequently they introduce words into their readers such as 'here' and 'what' as look/say words.

This method was embodied in the *Royal Road Readers* and the authors conducted controlled experiments to test its efficiency, first with non-readers in the junior school and later with infant school children. The efficiency of their method is given great support from this research where the phonic word method was compared with what is commonly termed 'mixed methods', i.e. an approach which included both 'whole-word' and 'phonic' methods. The improvements of the phonic word groups reported, particularly in the junior school experiment were vastly superior to those of the mixed methods group.

In the use of this approach together with the *Royal Road Readers,* I have found it necessary to add a good amount of practice material for the gradation of the books appears rather too steep in the early stages. There also seemed to be a danger of the children learning both sounds and words without acquiring a technique of allying one to the other.

Chall (1967) has suggested that the most promising approach to intial reading teaching seems to be through a method embodying a modified linguistic approach with one based on language experience. In other words the linguistic approach would provide for a definite growth structure in a knowledge of the spelling and grammatical usage of the language while the child's enthusiasm, interests and his own spoken language would bring realism and vitality to the reading process. Daniels and Diack have produced a modified linguistic approach in the *Royal Road Readers* and this could be a model for future developments.

Further reading

DANIELS, J. C. and DIACK, H. (1956) *Progress in Reading* University of Nottingham

DANIELS, J. C. and DIACK H. (1960) *Progress in Reading in the Infant School* University of Nottingham

DIACK, H. (1965) *In Spite of the Alphabet* Chatto and Windus

FLESCH, R. (1955) *Why Johnny Can't Read* Harper and Row

The Programmed Reading Kit

This approach was based in the thoughts and expcrience of a number of teachers working with D. H. Stott at Bristol University. It was first designed as an aid for illiterate youths and non-readers in the secondary school but has more recently been used with some success in infant schools. Experiments commenced in 1954 but the full kit became available as recently as 1962 and was revised in 1970.

Theoretically the scheme was based on two factors:

1. By programming the introduction of sounds and skills for their use, the child is enabled to learn at his own rate.

2. To restrict the vocabulary of reading books to phonically graded work inevitably results in too steep a gradation of difficulty or in text lacking in interest and motivation.

Stott set out, therefore, to devise a set of materials which would impart phonic knowledge and encourage the growth of phonic skills and yet at the same time be independent of reading books. As there was to be no story element to catch the child's interest the material was organized into individual and group games which are largely self-corrective.

It would be impossible here to describe each of the steps involved and the various games that are employed—such a description can be found in Stott's own handbook. Rather I will point a few comments which have become apparent when using the kit.

The kit does not replace reading books although its use alone for a period of time might well be justified in the case of a child who has a long history of failure with more traditional approaches. It was designed as a method of training children in the use of phonic skills, indeed Stott himself has written two series of readers which can be usefully used alongside the kit.

The value of reading games has often been questioned and some experimental evidence appears to show that such reading aids have little effect upon reading growth. This kit is rather more extensive and more scientifically planned that the usual type of reading game and there is also the challenge to the child to progress to the next stage in the scheme which does not exist in an odd game of word-lotto.

Daniels and Diack consider the sounding of letters to be too abstract an activity during the early stages of reading. Stott, however, builds a system of word analysis and synthesis into his scheme. He endeavours through the use of pictures to teach the most common sounds of each letter and then links a consonant and vowel together. Stott feels it essential that in such a word as 'bat' the child should learn to analyse it as 'ba-te' whereas others when teaching the child to link two letters would prefer to link the last two letters, i.e. 'be-at'. Stott argues strongly for his approach as being the one which is easiest for eye-movements and most realistic for the child. I prefer the latter method mainly on the grounds that it prevents the confusion caused by the unavoidable 'uh' sound attached to the final consonant.

I was surprised when I first discovered this material in use in an infant school, even though an amount of adaptation had been under-taken. The playing of many of the games requires an amount of maturity and sophistication not usually present in the five-year-old child, and therefore, more teacher help, often simply to explain the games themselves, would be required. I have found the material of great value in gaining phonic growth among young junior school children and for those of little reading attainment in the secondary school and would suggest it is more suitable in these areas.

Further reading
STOTT, D. H. (1962) *Programmed Reading Kit* Holmes
STOTT, D. H. (1964) *Roads to Literacy* Holmes

Programmed reading
In recent years there has been an appreciable growth in the use of programmed texts and types of teaching machines for the teaching of the initial stages of reading. So far in this country their use has been mainly with older children who have failed to make a start on the reading process during the infant school years. Much success has been reported, however, and with adaptation and imaginative integration of the work there seems no reason why the schemes produced should not prove equally successful with children of five years of age. Certainly the teacher need have no fear of letting the child loose with an expensive machine.

Such schemes have the advantage of providing carefully graded individual work through an interesting and exciting medium and the teacher is able to give individual help to the children with greater ease and effect. Enterprising teachers have developed many types of aid to make such a situation possible, e.g. the use of tape recorders, work books, filmstrips, stethoscopes and teaching machines. Below we will look at one of the commercial approaches, The Sullivan Associates' *Programmed Reading* books. One final point worthy of note is that at present, at least, if you wish to use programmed work you must be in sympathy with a predominantly phonic approach.

Cynthia Dee Buchanan *Programmed Reading* (Sullivan Associates: obtainable in this country through McGraw-Hill Publishing Company Ltd.)
This is an extensive scheme of programmed texts and accompanying story readers with a very gradual growth based almost entirely upon the phonic complexity of words. Before using the scheme the child should be familiar with the names and sounds of certain letters and be able to print them. He must also recognize the words 'yes' and 'no', be able to read from left to right and know that groups of letters form words. The books were first designed in America but were experimented with under the supervision of three British Universities before they were made freely available in this country. These trials, however, were far too short and possibly for this reason the books appeared more helpful than normal texts. Some good results have been reported after the use of this material but as yet its

use has mainly been confined to the remedial situation. I have only been able to observe the scheme in use in one infant school and, therefore, my comments are not based on any wide knowledge. The teacher will probably feel as I did on first seeing the books that the stilted, often ridiculous language would be valueless. In the school setting I found that the children thought funny, what had appeared ridiculous to me. I remain uncertain, however, as to whether the children will enjoy this type of medium for long. The approach in these books owes something to the move towards a linguistic approach though the authors use the term visuo-phonic method. I fear that in use such an approach could take us back to the pure phonic work of some 50 years ago.

My feeling here is that the basic idea is good but that it has been too fully worked out in the texts. It would have been better had more been left to the individual teacher, for supplementary work and teacher involvement is most necessary, even in the best devised programme for use with young children. Again our children, perhaps unlike the American equivalents enjoy small books through which they can pass speedily to a new text and gain an added stimulus to future progress.

For the individual teacher wishing to experiment the programmed text is one of the more fruitful channels of activity for in the devising and the use of such a text the teacher gets nearer to understanding the difficulties of the materials and the needs of the child.

Language Master (Bell and Howell)
This machine has been devised to enable a child working away from the teacher to increase his reading efficiency by relating sound and printed language, and in some cases a picture, to each other. The machine is in fact a two track tape recorder which plays tape bonded onto card. Thus a picture, word or letter can be put before the child as he hears the appropriate sound. The child runs the card through the machine until he feels he has mastered the work then switches the machine to the second track and makes what he feels is the correct response. The teacher will break any work given into small sets of cards and when these are completed can quickly check the work by playing it back.

Material specially designed for use with the machine includes cards to accompany the *Ladybird Key Words Reading Scheme*, the Word Study Kit which is an extensive phonic scheme and a set of beginning reading materials, the *Merry-go-round* scheme.

One of the chief virtues of the machine however is that the teacher can quickly make up sets of individual work on blank cards which can be purchased or even made from an old tape by an enthusiast. Thus phonic work, the introduction of new words, sentence completion exercises and work in visual and auditory discrimination can be worked out to cater for the needs of the individual child. The blank cards can be used over and over again for different items of work by simply fitting them with plastic pockets at the corners so that the picture and/or word section appears on a separate piece of card and is slipped in and then the new sound can be recorded in a matter of seconds.

This machine would seem to be a helpful aid in that the teacher can extend the amount of individual work given to any one child without denying another her attention. Again unlike many modern audio-visual aids, material can be teacher designed for the needs of the particular children.

Taped schemes
Over the past few years the tape recorder has increasingly become a prominent item of school equipment and its use in the sphere of reading is great. Apart from commercially produced schemes it is comparatively simple for the teacher to programme material for specific purposes or needs among her pupils. The possible uses are endless. Auditory discrimination, phonic work, language development exercises, speech training, comprehension, listening skills, the introduction of new words, guided workbook exercises or simply reading a book together with the tape are all possibilities and no doubt there are many more. Thus a tape recorder for individual work or adapted to take a multiple outlet for group work can be a boon to the busy teacher trying desperately to spread her attention to all her children. Some teachers may prefer to use tape playback units which have the advantage that the material cannot be wiped off accidentally.

Recently there has been a considerable growth in commercially produced tapes. Some reading schemes now have helpful tapes to increase the general efficiency of the scheme. There are also a number of special taped schemes mainly devised for remedial work but many could be used equally well in the infants school.

The Remedial Supply Company have a number of series of tapes for pre-reading, oral comprehension, language development, auditory discrimination and phonic work. Each series has accompanying books, workbooks or work sheets which enable the teacher quickly to check the efficiency of the learning. I have experimented with four- and five-year-old children using some of these schemes and have found that with careful usage the impetus given to early reading among even such children was considerable.

A number of sets of tapes and workbooks on cards for phonic work are available. The Remedial Supply Company has already been mentioned in this regard but more recently two further schemes have appeared. The Clifton Audio Visual Scheme (ESA) covers most of the normal work in phonics undertaken in schools by guided work involving workbooks. These are designed for remedial work but are not quite as stimulating as they could be for the exercises are of an identical nature throughout.

The most recent scheme and perhaps the most carefully prepared is that produced by Moseley under the title *English Colour Code Worksheets and Tapes* (National Society for Mentally Handicapped Children Centre for Learning Disabilities 1970). The words used are based on a number of studies into the vocabulary of children's books and the normal conversation of children whilst the order in which the letter/sound combinations are introduced is based on a computer analysis of their frequency within words. Colour cues are used for the vowel sounds so that the sound appears in the same colour throughout the worksheets no matter how the sound is represented in print. The names of the colours actually contain within them the vowel sound for which they are used; for instance the short 'e' sound is printed in red and the long 'e' in green. Interest in the material is sustained by cartoon drawings and rhymes and sound effects on tape. There are 20 hours of tapes and 60 worksheets which are produced on a coated card which can be wiped clean after use without leaving any indentation in the surface. Many children will no doubt gain great help from this scheme under the guidance of remedial teachers but it is not suitable for work in the infant school. It is also rather disappointing that after so much groundwork the worksheet activities have been allowed to be somewhat stereotyped and traditional in concept.

Teachers using taped schemes must ensure that they check on the work done orally from time to time for the accurate completion of the work cards is no guarantee that the ground covered has indeed been mastered. Often the child can learn sounds and even techniques of applying his knowledge but will not use these in wider reading activities unless the value and necessity is consciously pointed out.

Scott-Foresman Reading Systems

The Scott-Foresman Reading Systems were simultaneously published in America and the United Kingdom in 1970. They represent the largest range of matched reading materials published to date. The materials are divided into twelve stages each of which contains a wide variety of activities.

The materials are based on the acknowledgment that children learn in different ways, have different interests and that reading is not an isolated skill but something to be learned by being used, and because it is useful.

Each stage consists of matched modules of materials and no one child is likely to use or need to use every part of any given stage. The child who prefers factual reading and the child who likes stories can cover roughly the same ground in the development of reading skill within the area of his preference. Separate materials cover the development of comprehension and word study and materials are provided for literature and drama work as well as work in the content areas. In conception the scheme is admirable, but in production it is rather too formal; the skill-learning is overemphasized and there is a certain sameness in the presentation of the materials. Nevertheless it represents a considerable advance and gives much more freedom to both child and teacher than does the traditional reading scheme.

Further reading

CHALL, J. (1967) *Learning to Read: The Great Debate* McGraw-Hill

MOYLE, D. and MOYLE L. M. (1970) *Modern Innovations in Reading Teaching* United Kingdom Reading Association

ROBINSON, H. M. (Ed) (1968) *Innovation and Change in Reading Instruction* NSSE

SMITH, N. B. (1965) *American Reading Instruction* IRA

SOUTHGATE, V. and ROBERTS, G. R. (1970) *Reading: Which Approach?* ULP

VILSCEK, E. (Ed) (1968) *A Decade of Innovations* IRA

CHAPTER 6

Basic principles

We have examined the nature of language and endeavoured to appraise the manner in which a child learns to read. An attempt has been made to place before the reader an analysis of methods and media both past and present in order to portray their strengths and weaknesses and to discover what conclusions have been drawn from research projects. The reader will have noted the incomplete nature of our knowledge of the manner in which children learn to read, despite the fact that reading is probably the most researched area of human learning.

One of the reasons for this incomplete knowledge is the essentially individual nature of learning habits, influenced as they are by variations in ability, temperament and environment. The teacher also has qualities that are individual to her and as teaching involves the interplay of gifts and personalities between pupil and teacher, a further complication thus arises. The teacher therefore is in the best position to judge which facets of the various methods are likely to be most effective for her and her pupil at any given moment in time.

Having acknowledged this, it is equally true that we can infer a series of principles which would appear to form a good framework within which the teacher can select a variety of approaches and materials. In mapping out a set of principles for the design of a reading programme we must have an aim to guide our thinking. It is too easy to say that we want our children to become 'good', 'skilful', 'fluent' or 'complete' readers, for no two of us would agree upon the exact definitions of these adjectives. Let us therefore consider the traits evinced by a good reader in adult life, for it is necessary to have before us a view of the finished product if we are to proceed effectively. The marks of a good reader would seem to be fourfold.

1. The good reader enjoys reading

Reading is universally admitted to be a most useful skill yet although the majority of adults are reasonably fluent and practise the skill regularly, not nearly so many would confess to enjoying reading for its own sake. Reading can offer so much more than mere utilitarian advantages for it can, even to the unskilled, be enjoyable and to the skilled an exciting, stimulating yet relaxing activity. The truly literate adult does enjoy reading and from his reading increases not only his knowledge but also his aesthetic appreciation and the quality of his emotional life. Those who do not enjoy reading for pleasure, cut themselves off from a pursuit which could greatly enlarge their horizons and lift the quality of their mental and emotional life onto a higher plane.

2. The good reader is expert in word recognition techniques

All reading has its basis in the recognition of symbols. For the young child the unit of recognition may be the letter or single word but for the adult it will be the phrase. The good reader must be so expert in this skill that it becomes an almost unconscious, automatic activity for unless this stage is reached, fluency, comprehension and pleasure in reading will be greatly diminished.

3. The good reader reads with understanding

No one enjoys reading material which is incomprehensible, but reading with understanding implies much more than absorbing knowledge from the printed page. The good reader responds to the material read. He interprets new facts against the background of his previously accumulated knowledge and evaluates opinions given, by exercising his powers of judgement upon them. The reader in these terms is engaged in an interplay of his own thoughts and feelings with those expressed by the author. Reading is no longer a passive pursuit but an active and reactive process where two minds and two sets of experiences combine to produce new thoughts and new actions.

4. The good reader can adapt his reading technique to different purposes

The reading of a novel, a classical play or a science textbook, all require a different approach if the reader is to gain the maximum benefit from each. Along with the type of material, the purpose for which the material is being read will combine to determine the technique most appropriate to the task.

The good reader therefore is one who is able to skim for relevant facts, speed read to gain the gist of an argument and study to gain all the knowledge from any given passage.

The basic principles upon which a good reading programme should be based must be viewed firstly from the point of view of the nature of literacy at the adult level and secondly from that of the needs and abilities of the child at any given stage of development. The present writer looking at the problem from these two viewpoints suggests the following principles should be borne in mind.

Reading should form as natural a unit of the child's development as is possible
Reading being a product of civilization is not something which the child would gain if left entirely to his own devices. It comes therefore in rather a different category to physical growth, eating and walking. Its importance is much less evident to the child than is the ability to communicate through speech and yet one must still insist that for the achievement of success in reading, the whole activity must be as natural a part as possible of the child's development. The child's first experience of the printed word must be a natural one, though it will always be necessary to view our instruction against the total developmental pattern exhibited by the individual child.

If reading is to be an activity which appears natural to the child then any instruction given or attainment expected should be firmly based in a knowledge and understanding of the child's abilities and interests. Nor will it be sufficient simply to know an IQ score or a reading age but rather to be aware of the speed at which, and the directions in which the child's various abilities are developing. It is evident that for effective reading teaching we must know our children well and keep a record of events which are felt to reveal ability and personality growth. We have seen that reading is a most complex process and involves the use of many skills and abilities but one of these abilities, namely language facility deserves special mention. If reading is to be meaningful and enjoyable then we must be certain that the words which the child is called upon to read are words within his own vocabulary. It will be necessary to observe the child's use of language in normal conversation to check his width of vocabulary and his ability to express his ideas clearly in reasonably well constructed sentences. Whatever the stage of reading growth, whether the child is an absolute beginner or whether some fluency has been achieved, the reading programme must always be backed by a scheme for the growth of all language arts, for the extension of vocabulary and sensitivity to meaning and expression. Language facility is often seriously limited by a poor environment and therefore the teacher must be ready to create compensatory activities to help those children who are deprived of a satisfactory background.

As reading is a skill which children can master only slowly it must always be presented in a vital and interesting fashion. Often the interest of children in reading has to be kindled after they enter school. This should present little difficulty to the enthusiastic and resourceful teacher who will, by the provision of an exciting classroom atmosphere, be able to harness the natural energy and curiosity of the young child. Once the thirst for knowledge and the interest in books has been established then the development of reading attainment over the years will be largely ensured.

Reading as an integral part of other activities
The child must be led to an understanding that reading is useful and important. This will be achieved if he recognizes reading as a further and wider form of communication than is the spoken word. It is of little use expecting the child to look forward to the future. He feels only his present needs and thus even the very earliest steps must be seen to be vital to his present needs and interests. Consequently much of the beginnings of reading will be almost incidental as the child tries to make permanent the thought or feeling which is most powerfully present in his own mind at the time. As some attainment is gained his attention can be drawn to books which deal with the topic that interests him. Later still he can endeavour to send information and receive information on the same subject from another child who has a similar interest. Teachers frequently notice that the young child soon recognizes words commonly seen in television advertisements, on street signs and in shop windows but seems to take longer to master the seemingly simpler words of his primer. The reason is obvious, the one is part of his exciting experience the other not necessarily so. Two lessons can be learned here, namely the importance of revising our ideas as to which words the child can most usefully meet in print at the early stages of learning to read and further the necessity of incorporating reading as an integral part of activities to which the child will respond through interest and curiosity. The divorce of reading from other subjects in the curriculum is to be deplored for it makes for an unnatural and mechanical situation in which the only stimuli left for the child are the desire to

please teacher and the social pressures which communicate to the child that the ability to read is a status symbol.

Reading instruction should be attractive to the child
Young children love to talk and enjoy listening to stories. Why then do so many find reading unattractive and make little or no progress? It may be that instruction started too early or the child was subjected to an inappropriate approach. Certainly the number of children who find difficulty in learning to read would be greatly reduced if in the early stages they found enjoyment and success. It should be possible to ensure that all reading instruction is an enjoyable activity in its own right for all our children even when ability or environment decrees that progress will be slow.

All reading should be meaningful
Under this general heading are a number of points. It is obviously important that the child should be capable of understanding the material he is asked to read. Thus the vast majority of words, and in the early stages all words, should be within the child's spoken vocabulary. It is perhaps a little less obvious that we should also insist on the books the child is given being meaningful in their own right. Many of our existing primers fail in this respect for often the text has no meaning and any real content has to be inferred from a study of the illustrations.

e.g. Come, come, Rover.

Such words can convey little and it is not sufficient that the picture shows a boy calling to a dog. If we expect our children to comprehend what is read then we must ensure that the material we ask them to read is worthy of the mental effort involved.

A third point here is one which seems to be most often overlooked. It must be emphasized that children must have some explanation of the value of the activity they are asked to do, that they understand how it will aid their progress and also see its place in the scheme of instruction. So often many of the games and phonic activities, which children engage in, have little effect because the children have not seen the relationship between them and their reading books and consequently never employ the skills gained when meeting the need for them in their storybooks.

Word recognition skills cannot be ignored
Whilst every effort must be made to ensure that reading is enjoyable, that it is integrated with other work, fitted to the interests of the

child and uses to the full his creative abilities, maximum growth in reading will only be achieved if attention is also paid to the more mechanical aspects of reading. A definite scheme for the improvement of visual and auditory discrimination, orientation, phonic knowledge and techniques must be employed which will lead finally to skill in syllabification and phrase reading. Though the nature and timing of such instruction will depend on the attributes of the individual child, it is wise to commence it at the earliest possible moment in the individual child's development. It must be remembered however that the needs of children for instruction of this type will vary and that when it is given it should be presented in an attractive manner.

Instruction should lead increasingly to independence in reading
It is often noted that the young child reads much more fluently within the reading scheme he is used to than in any other book of comparable difficulty. It is not our purpose here to go into all the reasons for this, but simply to stress that to confine the child to one reading scheme without the provision of other reading experiences is not helpful in promoting growth of independence in reading. The more a child reads, the more he should be able to read without help. On the other hand if we are to give the child every help to become completely independent we must make sure that the help that we give is going to have this result. It will be commonly acknowledged that the child will need some instruction in word recognition techniques and in the basic skill of comprehension. At a later stage he will need instruction in how his reading technique can be adapted to the particular purpose for which he is reading. It is perhaps worth mentioning here that children can be given too much help. Many, for example, believe that when the child in reading a story meets an unknown word he should be told it immediately or fluency and interest may be lost. This is not necessarily so and if the child is to become an independent reader he must on occasions be directed to use the word recognition skills which he has been given.

Every activity must be related to the whole scheme
It is not usual to send a gardener into the desert to learn his craft, yet so often one sees children in reading lessons undertaking tasks which are totally unrelated and unhelpful to their progress in reading. Any activity which a child undertakes must fit in with the aims of

the reading programme as a whole and bear a logical relationship to previous activities and hoped-for future development.

Progress through the reading programme must be kept under review

The teacher, particularly if the class is large, will find it difficult to ensure that all the children are achieving a satisfactory rate of reading growth. Again there is also the problem of keeping the programme in line with the individual strengths and weaknesses of the children.

To achieve the necessary evaluation of the individual child's progress it will be necessary to keep detailed records of work done and errors made and occasionally to administer some form of standardized test. When any child appears to be having any sort of difficulty a check should be made of his records and suitable diagnostic tests administered in order that a reappraisal of his reading programme may be made.

In conclusion it cannot be overemphasized that the child learns the skills of reading by using them. It will sometimes be necessary to isolate some skill activity for specific practice in order to maintain progress. When this is done the child should realize the necessity for the activity and exactly how and where it is going to help him. Periods of mechanical work, when necessary, should be brief and immediately followed by the use of the skill in a realistic reading situation, otherwise there is the danger that the child may acquire the skill but will not apply it in his normal approach to reading.

Further reading
MERRITT, J. E. (Ed) (1971) *Reading and the Curriculum* Ward Lock Educational

CHAPTER 7

Major approaches to teaching reading

In any discussion of the teaching of reading one topic sure to crop up is the merits of various approaches to beginning reading. It is obvious that all the viewpoints involve major assumptions and all too often unexamined prejudices. Many teachers believe implicitly in one particular approach in spite of substantial evidence from research and observation that no one method of teaching the early reading skills is outstandingly superior. For an individual teacher and child one approach may be much more effective than any other but what is of real importance is the expertise of the teacher and the attitudes and abilities of the child.

Any theoretical description of approaches to reading is hardly likely to correspond exactly to the way an individual teacher harnesses that approach in the classroom. This makes research into the effectiveness of approaches extremely difficult. Furthermore the majority of teachers employ a 'mixed methods' approach using elements drawn from more than one approach. However the selection of approaches, and the time and emphasis given to each section, varies so much from teacher to teacher that the term itself is meaningless without a supplementary description of the elements and their weighting. All too often the discussion of approaches will degenerate into an argument between those who favour a whole approach and those who favour a phonic approach. This controversy has dragged on for many years and seems pointless. To look at beginning reading in either of these terms alone is to isolate those elements which are concerned solely with mechanical word recognition from the full reading process.

There are three major elements to be considered—the child, the teacher and the nature of the reading process. Each of these three will interact with the others to suggest a possible solution to the task of fitting all three together in order to achieve success for the individual child. We must examine each of these elements before we can make an appraisal of the advantages and weaknesses of the various approaches.

The child

Each child has his own unique balance of abilities, experiences, previous learning, personality and interests and all these elements need consideration. In deciding which approach is to be given the most weighting at any given moment in time, the following questions need to be explored.

1. Do the child's emotional and personality characteristics suggest he will benefit more from formal or informal approaches? There is a certain amount of evidence to suggest that children who tend to be withdrawn or anxious have more success with formal, teacher-directed approaches than more informal ones.

2. What are the respective strengths of the child's visual and auditory perceptions? Some approaches make heavier demands on one than the other, though of course both are involved in all approaches.

3. What level of oral language development has been reached?

4. What is the child's age and level of general ability?

5. Has the child any particular interests which can be identified with the materials of a given approach?

The teacher

1. What is the teacher's general philosophy of education? Does she prefer a formal teacher-directed approach or an informal and child-centred approach?

2. Is a highly systematic or incidental teaching approach preferred?

3. Does she feel that reading should be isolated from work in the other language arts?

For both teacher and child the answers to the above questions must be given, not only in terms of the teaching approach, but also with regard to the actual materials to be used. It is difficult to separate the two aspects in the practical situation, but in planning the framework upon which a reading programme is to be based, it is essential to consider the strengths and weaknesses of each approach at a theoretical level. If this is not done, the gaps or weaknesses of a given approach may not be realized.

Criteria for the selection of an approach to beginning reading

1. To what extent does the approach give help in mastering the primary or beginning reading skills? These include:

a. The association of spoken and printed language.

b. The awareness of a correspondence between the left to right letter order within words and the sequence of sounds within a word.

c. The ability to differentiate between letter shapes.

d. The relationship of symbol to sound.

e. Strategies for decoding unfamiliar words.

f. The understanding that printed language gives a message or information.

2. Does the approach have any elements which may hamper later learning? For example an approach which overemphasizes word analysis may prevent fluent reading later if the child cannot shake off the habit of examining each individual letter carefully before making a response.

3. Does the approach encourage the child to become an independent reader as quickly as possible? How soon can the child use his skill freely in a variety of reading situations?

4. Does the approach emphasize the mechanical skills of reading or the understanding of the content of what is read?

5. Does the approach encourage or discourage thoughtful and critical examination of the content of books?

6. How natural, realistic and useful an activity will reading appear to the child?

Major approaches to beginning reading teaching

Most of the major approaches to reading teaching have been described and discussed in Chapters 2 and 5, but it will be useful here to summarize them and reexamine their major strengths and weaknesses.

Alphabetic

Here the child learns to recognize letters and spell out words using letter names. The approach emphasizes recognition of words rather than the meaning conveyed by print. It seems to be helpful with spelling and left/right orientation, but letter names are not particularly helpful and are often unrelated to the sound value. The child may lose interest in reading when concentrating solely on letter recognition.

Further a learning set may be established by this detailed attention to letters which may limit reading with anticipation at a later date.

Traditional phonic
This group of approaches has as its unifying factor the sounding out of the individual letters in a word and blending the sounds to make the word. It is useful in tackling words not recognized by sight when the correct word cannot be gained from contextual clues, or for checking the accuracy of the choice of word on the basis of such clues. Phonic work can be carefully structured, and systematically taught. Many children find this approach difficult unless substantial work in the development of auditory discrimination and thinking strategies involved has been undertaken. The method demands the type of thinking which Piaget claims is present in the period of 'concrete operations' which the average child has not attained by the age of 5 years. The irregularity of English spelling restricts the realism of vocabulary in early readers and the number of rules which have to be memorized is excessive if the method is to be used to cover the whole of English spelling. There is also the danger of an emphasis upon letter and word recognition at the expense of reading for meaning. In common with other systematic approaches it is difficult to make full use of the child's own language which results from other activities in the classroom.

Visuo-phonic and linguistic approaches
These approaches are based in a recognition that the sound value given to letters sounded in isolation is generally different from the contribution the letter makes to the sound of the total word. The child learns to respond to groups of letters from the beginning. This is more realistic and unifies some of the better features of phonic and whole word methods. It is still subject to the difficulties mentioned above concerning reading for meaning and applicability to other work, as spelling patterns are progressively taught moving from the simple and regular to increasingly complex and irregular.

Whole-word and look/say approaches
These approaches depend upon the memorization of words by their configuration. Learning is by association of words with pictures and joining words such as 'the' and 'here' by such means as flash cards. Books used in this area tend to be repetitive and in the early stages words are often chosen for the difference they present as patterns. The approach does have the advantage of being less

restricting than the more systematic methods reviewed above for words which children meet in other contexts can be used. It seems to function well in the very early stages but as all new words have to be visually memorized the learning load soon becomes too great. The child has to wait to be told any new word by the teacher and as such the approach restricts reading independence.

Story method
This consists in children reading stories, or summaries of stories, which have previously been read to them. In the early stages this gives a great sense of success and satisfaction in that unrecognized and difficult words can often be tackled from memory of the story which has been read. It gives the child the ability to respond to meaning from the beginning, but from a growth point of view has all the limits imposed by memorization and a lack of ability to deal with words not previously met in print.

Individualized reading
This is not really a pure approach but is characterized by the child's freedom to choose any book to read, at any time, by the writing of book reports and discussion with the teacher. The teacher will often add to this approach some group work in phonics. The approach fits well with the individual interests of children and emphasizes reading for meaning, but few children are able to begin learning to read without some further help. Growth will depend to some extent upon the aspects of other approaches which are included, but the regular intervention of the teacher ensures that work undertaken is apposite and interesting, and enables the child to appreciate the need for learning any particular skills or techniques.

Language-experience approaches
Teaching strategies under this heading are employed to some extent by most teachers, but form the major approach to reading in some schools. Again it is not a pure approach but will usually involve aspects of some of the approaches already described.

In practice it varies from the encouragement of children to talk about themselves, their experiences and ideas, later recording them in writing; to the situation where the teacher involves groups of children in some learning activity where the need for reading and writing can be appreciated and become rewarding. In essence it is the most natural and realistic approach and the child learns to read by using his reading. This overcomes to some extent the difficulty of motivating the child to engage in devised activities in order to learn the subskills of the reading process and the problem of obtaining transfer of these skills to 'real' reading situations. The teacher will find however that very careful recording and some teaching of the subskills are necessary to achieve maximum reading growth. We must beware of the possibility of placing children in problem-solving situations before they have attained the skills necessary to solve the problem. The teacher must be aware therefore of the nature of the learning involved in any given activity which children are asked to undertake.

Eclectic or mixed method approaches
It will be clear by now that no one approach appears to satisfy all the criteria that were set. Chall (1967) reviewing sixty-seven major researches into the various approaches to reading did not find any evidence, in the standards achieved, that any one pure approach was in practice more successful than any of the others.

The vast majority of teachers are aware of this and use a mixture of approaches whatever media or materials form the basis of their reading programme.

The chief danger of mixed methods is that the child can so easily become confused. Teachers too often expect far more from incidental teaching of say phonics than this type of teaching can hope to produce. It would seem that mixed methods will only work really efficiently if the mixing is carefully planned and the work integrated.

Chall proposed the mixture of a highly structured, e.g. linguistic, approach with a meaning approach such as language experience work.

A suggested approach
The following suggestion for planning work among young children is a personal one based on the author's experience. It is offered as a guideline to thinking rather than a syllabus to be followed. Each teacher must examine themselves, their children and their situation, before working out a plan of their own.
1. Introduction to reading. This assumes that visual, auditory and linguistic development is at the normal 5 year old level.
a. Reading pictures and picture stories, anticipating outcomes.
b. Reading caption books with the help of a tape.

c. Story method.

d. Conversation based on experiences and the production of group books.

e. Compiling a personal picture dictionary.

f. Learning the most common sound value of letters—not as the first step in a traditional phonic approach but so that the child can be helped to use this knowledge as a check on the recognition of words by contextual clues.

2. Development in the second and third years of the infant school.

a. A progressive scheme for the introduction of a knowledge of the spelling patterns of English.

b. The use of a good reading scheme or sets of books graded by the teacher so that the child can select books which interest him within a limited area of difficulty.

c. Provision of a wide range of books for free choice reading.

d. Language experience work at individual and group level.

e. Reading-thinking activites.

Items c to e above make provision for the acquisition of reading to take place in relation to the other language arts and the content areas of the curriculum, thus stressing the uses and significance of printed and written material.

The activities listed above will be further explained later in the volume.

Further reading
CHALL, J. (1967) *Learning to Read: The Great Debate* McGraw-Hill
SOUTHGATE, V. and ROBERTS, G. R. (1970) *Reading—Which Approach?* ULP
STAUFFER, R. G. (1969) *Learning to Read as a Thinking Process* Harper and Row

PART THREE

Day to day work within the classroom

CHAPTER 8

Matters of organization

In order that growth in reading ability can proceed at the best possible rate it is necessary to give some thought to the organization of our instruction. Unless there is definite and thoughtful planning then the children will be allowed to waste time and possibly become bored. The teacher will also not be able to make the best use of the time available, considering the heavy pressures of an ever expanding curriculum and the numbers of children within her class.

The first and most obvious question from the planning point of view is—Where shall we timetable the reading period?

Historically it was thought that work in the basic skills should be allocated during the morning session. Mathematics was generally given pride of place for it was deemed that children were more capable of the mental gymnastics involved at this time. English work under such headings as reading, comprehension and composition generally occupied the time between morning break and lunch; the afternoon being mainly allocated to more practical pursuits. More recently infant and some junior schools have time-tabled a block of time, again usually in the morning session, for activities in the basic skills and the individual teacher has been left to divide this time up according to her own desires and the children's needs. The advantages of timetabling are obvious; the head-teacher and class-teacher know what time is available and that instruction is being given regularly. The child also has a certain amount of security in knowing what is going to be expected of him at any given time. The weaknesses of this type of organization lie in the limitations which are imposed. Reading tends to become separated from many of the activities of which it is an essential part. The assignment card given in mathematics may completely ignore the standard of attainment reached by the child in reading, written work becomes divorced from reading and the interest and motivation gained from the content and practical subjects may never be transferred to the reading process. In this situation many children never see the usefulness of reading as an aid to learning, as a means of communication or as an excellent medium for satisfying one's curiosity, but view reading as an end in itself which for many children is insufficient cause to expend their mental energy. The integrated curriculum is therefore to be commended for the vitality and interest which it can bring to the child and his work. It is not without its weaknesses however for it will always be difficult to find sufficient time to give individual children the help which they need and it is noted that when schools are organized in this way the mechanical side of reading is often ignored and as a result some children fail to make progress. It would seem therefore that in general terms there should be no need in the infant school to have a timetabled period for reading, provided that the teacher can make available the time for group and individual work. Often when children are following group or individual projects the teacher can in fact find more time for this individual work, for with careful organization the children can work for fairly long periods without teacher involvement and individuals or groups can be withdrawn for instruction in reading at intervals throughout the whole day. It must be stressed however that such an approach can only be successful when the teacher is prepared to spend a good deal of time outside school hours on the preparation of the work and also keeps detailed records of the children's work and progress. I would feel that the integrated approach can only be workable in the infant school when classes have a maximum size of 25 pupils.

Classwork

The approach wherein the whole class is given the same book and one child at a time reads in turn has largely fallen into disuse. The reasons for this are that it would seem an unrealistic approach, for few children are likely to be at the same stage in reading attainment or all share a common interest in one single text. Again it would appear uneconomical, for only one child is reading and thus only one child's difficulties are being examined while the rest of the class are playing the more passive role of following the text—if in fact they are engaged in any mental activity at all. When demand for books usually exceeds supply it is unwise to purchase sets of forty or more copies of the same book. Again the simple act of reading aloud brings its own complications. Most children read more quickly when reading silently and the child with a speech defect is not limited in fluency when he doesn't have to make a sound response. On the other hand reading aloud is an important skill for here the child comes to realize how important to the meaning of a passage are the variations in volume and pitch of voice. Vocal expression whether in conversation or in reading has been neglected in recent years and one can only hope that the recent emphasis on communication in schools will produce children with voices which are more pleasant and interesting to listen to, for then the meaning they wish to express will be more readily and accurately comprehended by the listener.

There must therefore be a place for reading aloud not only to the teacher but also before a large group. The most obvious place for this is through the media of drama and poetry which can only be truly appreciated when performed. Many other occasions present themselves however during the course of a school day. Children can take part in the school's act of corporate worship by reading passages of scripture and prayers. One child may have written some news which the teacher feels is of interest to the whole class so the child is called upon to read it. As groups of children complete projects on which they have been engaged they can present their work to the whole class reading the captions to the illustrations and any text which they have compiled.

Most of the work which the whole class engage in together will be in activities related to reading rather than reading to the rest of the class whilst classmates follow the same text. Under advantageous conditions of buildings and class numbers class lessons in reading would be infrequent but when faced with a very large class they can often be profitably increased. Perhaps the most frequent class activity in reading will be listening to the teacher read a story. This will be a daily feature of work throughout the infant school. Less frequently the class may be drawn together for guided writing practice, or the explanation of a new step in phonic work.

Group work

The activity where the class divides into groups of 4 to 6 children and read from the same text in turn is still quite common in the first two years of the junior school. The teacher usually moves from group to group or concentrates her time upon those children who are not making satisfactory progress. Sometimes groups are formed entirely of children who have approximately the same reading attainment or alternatively each group is given a leader whose reading attainment is superior to that of the group.

Dr Joyce Morris (1966) comments that, in the observations of reading instruction made during the preparation of the Kent Reading Survey, she and her colleagues felt group reading to be the least productive approach to the teaching of reading. It would seem that all the possible advantages of this method of instruction are better catered for by regular individual or silent reading and some class work as outlined above. The disadvantages are many and often I have observed lessons where the teacher spent more time and energy in keeping the children in their places and following the text than in helping them with their reading. I felt in fact that the major object was to exhibit the authority of the teacher. Disciplinary difficulties will always arise when the interests and abilities of the children are not being catered for. The width of interest and attainment even in a small group can be quite wide and some will limp through the book with great difficulty whilst another is impatiently wanting to race ahead. Reading speeds in children of equal attainment vary greatly and the child reading aloud usually falls behind those reading silently, for most people can read more quickly than they can speak. Thus the group situation lacks motivation, for the silent readers are waiting for the oral reader and soon begin to lose interest. The silent reading speed of the children will probably be reduced by constantly being held back. If a more able child is given the position of group leader he can only tell the child the word he does not know, he cannot devise activities to help the child memorize the word he does not know, nor can he keep a record of the help which any child needs. Further if the better readers are used in this way continuously we do them a great injustice by not providing material which will extend their own attainment. If the children are all of roughly the same attainment the only really valuable part of the lesson will be when they have the attention of the teacher.

Though group reading as outlined above would seem to have little value, division into groups for other activities involving and helpful to reading will be most advantageous particularly when large numbers within the class forbid individual contact with the teacher being as frequent as one would like. Small groups are admirable structures for interest and project work, for the introduction of a new step in phonic work, structured work in comprehension or for the use of reading apparatus and reading games. All too often these days reading is carried out entirely as an individual activity. However when opportunities are given for children to discuss their reading and written work there will be considerable growth in the understanding of the ground which has been covered. The children will begin to read with questions in mind, with anticipation, and be more thoughtful and critical of the information before them.

Individual work

Undoubtedly, in the early stages of reading, the most valuable single facet of a reading programme will be the moments when the child has the satisfaction of having the teacher's full attention for a few moments whilst he reads to her. The child feels important and cared for in this situation, whilst the teacher is able to supply immediately the type of encouragement or support which is needed. Though teaching machines, tape recorders and the like can cater to some extent for individual requirements they cannot and should not replace this type of situation. Such teacher-pupil contact should continue for all children throughout the infant and junior school stage and will remain helpful to many children during the secondary school stage. The frequency of this contact will lessen quite naturally as the child grows in fluency, but at the moment most teachers seem to drop this activity rather too early in the child's reading development.

Individual reading is not without weaknesses. It is a very time-consuming task and the treatment of individual difficulties on any large scale is perhaps an inefficient use of time. It is probably best to use this time for simply hearing the child read, then by careful recording of the child's needs, he can be set reading activities which he can work out on his own to satisfy these needs. Again a glance at the records might reveal three or four children who have a difficulty in common or are ready to be given a particular type of phonic instruction, word study or comprehension work. This should be noted and then executed with the group rather than being undertaken a number of times with individual children. Young children cannot work on an individual programme for long periods without the intervention and help of the teacher, but by the time the child has reached the junior school he should be able to undertake a good deal of work on an assignment basis leaving the teacher more able to concentrate on the teaching of new stages in the development of reading skills.

One area of individual work which is most important, yet for which no administrative structure should be necessary, is that of silent reading—the time when the child reads for his own pleasure. Here the giving of opportunity and an ample supply of books both good and attractive, covering a wide range of interests should provide sufficient stimulus.

Hearing the children read

It has already been intimated that the time when the child reads to the teacher is perhaps the most important part of reading instruction. The necessity of hearing children read regularly will decline as fluency increases but during the early stages it will be necessary to hear the children read every page of his book. (The child should of course have recourse to other books for silent reading purposes but the book referred to is that which is central to the scheme he is following.) This means that once the child has started upon a reading scheme the aim should be to hear him read a little every day. This is better than several pages every third or fourth day. One realizes of course that the infant teacher may be faced with the impossible task of trying to hear 30 or 40 children read each day. This would mean, even if it is possible, that there would be very little time for teacher involvement in the many other activities of the infant schoolroom with the result that children would probably be wasting a great deal of time and boredom would set in. There are of course a number of ways round this problem. Time available can be increased by carefully structured, self-corrective materials, provision of workbooks and games. Such aids as the Language Master and the tape recorder can be used to supplement individual contact between the teacher and the child. In the final analysis, however, the heavily pressed teacher will find that she will have to be content to hear only occasional pages from the children who are progressing well, in order to concentrate on those who are just beginning to read. Let us acknowledge however that this is often a compromise and that there are few children during the infant school years who would not benefit from daily contact of this type. A further idea often employed is to allow the child to take his book home and read to his parents. For this to be successful parents need to be instructed in what to do and how to do it, for all too often children find on taking home their books that parents are not sufficiently interested to give them the necessary time, or at the opposite end of the scale they become unsettled through their parents' anxiety for speed and success.

At the junior school stage the average reader in the first year should be heard read approximately every third day whilst for the average child in the fourth year once per week will be sufficient. The poorer reader will of course require more frequent help and the exceptionally good readers will rarely need to be heard by the time they are eleven years of age.

Hearing children read is valuable from many points of view:

1. The child usually enjoys having the teacher's full attention centred upon him for a few moments and this increases effort on his part.

2. The teacher can impart a feeling of success which the child may not experience when reading on his own.

3. The child can be helped to bring expression into his reading.

4. New words met can be discussed and added to the child's vocabulary.

5. The teacher can observe the progress being made by the child and therefore can follow up the sessions by providing materials which will promote further reading growth.

6. The teacher will note any difficulties being experienced and thus be able to devise activities to remedy them.

7. The teacher can keep a constant check on the child's understanding of what is read.

Every effort must be made to hear the children read as frequently as possible. It is perhaps worth a mention that if all reading were to be undertaken aloud the speed of comprehension in silent reading would probably be reduced. However with our present large classes I cannot envisage that teachers will have anywhere near enough time to make this a recognizable danger.

Hearing children read regularly is an admirable pursuit in its own right but its effectiveness is greatly increased if it is looked upon as a teaching situation, and full records are kept and made use of in the future.

In points 1 to 7 listed above are some pointers towards making this teacher-pupil contact effective and these will be elaborated later in this book. It should be noted that this is a teaching situation and as such the teacher is expected to instruct where necessary and not simply to sit and listen. Many teachers seem to treat this type of reading as a performance by the child and thus when the child comes to an unknown word they feel that fluency and comprehension have pride of place and supply the unknown word as quickly as possible. This would seem right in the reading of a play or a poem before a group or class but it is unhelpful and unrealistic in the teacher-pupil individual situation. Surely both fluency and comprehension have already received a setback at the moment of hesitation before the correct word was supplied and therefore it would seem advantageous to make use of the mistake to form a focal point for some brief instruction and then return to the beginning of the sentence to regain flow of reading and comprehension. Difficulties of word recognition can be looked upon as a problem-solving activity with the teacher gently guiding the child to the clues available following the general plan outlined in chapter 3. One would stress that if the child's reading programme has been carefully designed these breaks in reading should be few. Whenever a child comes anywhere near the error rate of one mistake in any ten running words the text is proving too difficult for him to memorize the new words being introduced.

Most infant school teachers keep some record of reading progress but this is not nearly so universal, unfortunately, in the junior school. For many these records go little further than a piece of card used by the child as a book-mark which shows the books read and which page or pages the child read on each occasion he was heard by the teacher. Such cards, providing they are not lost, serve a useful administrative and organizational purpose but are little help in gaining maximum reading progress for the child. Something a little more detailed is called for. A number of teachers are given to the procedure of using odd scraps of paper on which incidental phonic work is done during the session with the individual child. I would suggest that an amalgamation of the card and the odd scraps of paper form the basis of good record keeping. Thus each child could have a book which formed his own reading record and which could be kept during the whole of his passage through the school. This book would commence with a schedule, to be explained more fully in chapter 13, where results of reading attainments and diagnostic tests would be noted, together with any relative comments concerning environment, language development and the like. The remainder of the book would contain a record of his reading sessions and comments concerning written work, speech and special interests. This record can be quickly glanced at as the child comes up to read and considered in more detail when his individual reading programme is redesigned or when planning apparatus work, supplementary reading, word study and word recognition exercises.

The value of detailed recording is that it provides the teacher with a full picture of the child's development pattern which can be the only satisfactory basis for making decisions with regard to future planning. It avoids wasting time upon instruction and activities in areas already mastered by the child and points the teacher to profitable areas of instruction. So often teachers on hearing children read note a particular difficulty which the child is experiencing but because of lack of records and the pressure of work the same difficulty is noted time and again, forgotten and no remedial activity is provided.

Recording can become just a matter of keeping records and these are perhaps of minor historic value. The idea outlined above however is meant to be a central part of reading instruction being referred to and added to frequently and in the early stages of reading at least should be used on every individual reading occasion. Used in this way the record as a whole is a diagnostic document helpful to the planning for future progress at every stage. Teachers may feel that such detailed recording takes up far too much time for the helpfulness the task brings. This has not been so in the present writer's experience when working with large classes. I have found that most of the recording could be done whilst the child was reading so that little time was in fact lost in class, though I must admit that much of the analysis and decision-making as a result of items recorded had to be undertaken after school.

Below is a typical section taken from such a record in the case of a child who was making quite good progress.

Frank B. Calendar age 6 years 7 months   Reading age approx 8 years   *Janet and John* Book 4 Pages 65 to 67.
Preliminary work—discussion of fruits and the sound 'ea' as in peach.
(List of words compiled together with the child)
eat teach reach peat leaf
(Some difficulty in separating 'ee' from 'ea'.)
floating (Could not read this word and failed to analyse it correctly as sound 'oa' was not known—eventually gave correct response after discussion of the illustration—a peach floating in a stream.)
'found'—rather shaky (Not yet memorized though word has been met before—was able to analyse it phonically.)
'then' and 'they'—some confusion—carelessness?
Follow-up exercises on sounds 'ea' and 'oa'.

(Such exercises at a suitable level occur in Tansley's *Sound Sense* Book 6, or Murray's *Key Words Reading Scheme* Books 7c and 8c, also the game *Word Bits* produced by Galt.)

The words in brackets are added for the reader's benefit and do not appear in the original record.

A second example which appears below comes from the record of a child who was receiving remedial instruction.

David F. Calendar age 8 years 9 months Reading age 5 years 9 months *Racing to Read* Book 6 Page 10.

(Discussion of illustration on facing page which shows a caravan with a girl inside catching fire whilst other children and their pets run towards it.)

cat–catch–catches (Revision of these words which first appeared in Book 5.)

caravan and Carol confused (Evidence that the child is guessing words from their first few letters.)

'of' read for 'off'

'catches' (still hesitating over this word)

Making a rather large number of errors—extensive workbook activities needed. (An example of such activities is reproduced below.)

Missing words

Ruff jumps................the seat.

The door................the caravan is blue. ⎫ off

Carol takes her frock................. ⎬ or **?**

Can she get out................the fire. ⎭ of

Which things catch on fire?

Where does the caravan catch fire?

It................fire by the.................

Further reading

GARDNER, W. K. (1965) *Towards Literacy* Blackwell

MERRITT, J. E. (Ed) (1971) *Reading and the Curriculum* Ward Lock Educational

STAUFFER, R. G. (1970) *The Language Experience Approach to the Teaching of Reading* Harper and Row

CHAPTER 9

Getting them going

Individual schools and teachers vary greatly in their attitude as to how a beginning to the reading process should be made. Some teachers enter the reception class of the infant school on the first morning of a child's school life armed with the first book of the school's chosen reading scheme and expect all children to make an immediate start. At the other end of the scale we have some teachers who believe that the child will read when he is ready and so they simply wait for the child to commence teaching himself.

Both extreme points of view here are mistaken. The teacher's first task is to assess the physical and mental maturity of each child and having done this appropriate activities can be devised which will follow naturally from the stage of maturity reached and lead more certainly to later success.

Most infant school teachers are very good at getting to know their children but usually less adept or less interested in making a truly scientific appraisal of the child's abilities. Continuing careful observation is most necessary but it is given point and direction if considered alongside the results and observations which come from the use of readiness tests and diagnostic materials. Such tests cannot of course be used with young children until a good teacher-pupil relationship has been established. Observations and tests will quickly show up those children who have already started to read and those at the other end of the scale who are so lacking in ability, or so deprived of an educationally sound environment that reading a book is out of the question in the foreseeable future. They should also guide the teacher in selecting those activities which will be most helpful to promoting growth towards or in reading for all the children. The use and interpretation of readiness and diagnostic materials will be further discussed in chapters 14 and 15, here we are concerned with what practical help can be given to children in general, in order to encourage reading growth. It will also be noted that many of the activities mentioned below should be a continuing feature of the classroom environment if good progress is to be maintained.

The creation of a helpful classroom atmosphere

Children are very sensitive to the attitudes and personalities of adults and the enthusiastic and hardworking teacher will usually produce similar attributes among the children under her care. The children will want to please her, and consequently if the latter shows that she attaches value to reading then the children will desire to read.

The classroom should be an exciting place with lots of things to do, see and talk about. Interesting exhibits and pictures carefully captioned and regularly changed should always be present. There should be a plentiful supply of attractive books on display and their usefulness made obvious by directing the children to an illustration or by the teacher choosing one book to read a story to the children. The children should be allowed to help with the planning and organization of the classroom, the dispersal of furniture and the use of the available display spaces. The classroom situation should challenge and direct the children but also allow sufficient freedom for the development of individual interests and to encourage communication among the children.

Encouraging the development of spoken language

Reading should always be considered as part of the total scheme of language arts in which almost all our communication is based. These language arts are traditionally four in number, namely speech, listening, reading, and writing. To these however we might well add a fifth, namely thinking, for it has already been noted that the quality of our thought processes is closely related to our proficiency in the use of language for we think in language symbols.

It is possible therefore for a person to have five vocabularies which whilst having a common core of words and constructions vary in their extent and proficiency in use. These five are the vocabularies we use for speaking, listening, thinking, reading and writing. When the child first enters school there will already be established some level of competence in speaking, listening and thinking but probably little or no development of the reading and writing vocabularies. Historically it was considered that the task of the school was to concentrate upon reading and writing and these together with arithmetic came to be known as the 3 Rs or the basic educational skills. Consequently children at the top end of the secondary school were often capable of using far more words in a reading setting than they did in normal conversation. It is hoped that this division of the language arts and over concentration upon one area of development is now disappearing for we have realized that the development of vocabularies in speaking and listening are of supreme importance to reading with insight and understanding. Children under past regimes were able to make the correct mechanical responses to the printed word but often remained in complete ignorance of the shades of meaning many words were capable of having. It is also probable that the extent of vocabulary shown in conversational speech is that which is most closely related to our thought processes and thus to gain responsive reading and a thoughtful approach to all learning we must concentrate first upon extending the range and sensitivity of word usage in speech, the most natural area of communication. Before we can really help the child to enlarge his spoken vocabulary and his usage of English we must first have some knowledge of his maturity and expertise in these areas. Many young children enter school having lived in an environment which for five years has deprived them of what we would consider to be a normal linguistic background. Such children will need compensatory activities designed to meet their special needs and unless these are provided they will soon feel that school is lacking in interest and excitement. This sort of provision should not be difficult if the classroom atmosphere permits self expression and the teacher is willing to listen to the child's clumsy attempts to express himself in language.

The development of all the language arts must be based in experience. As these arts are all concerned with communication they will develop naturally when children are placed in an environment which is sufficiently interesting, exciting and stimulating that they feel they must tell others of the wonder and joy they have discovered. Thus the quality of discussion, conversation, reporting, interest and eventually reading and written work all bear a direct relationship to the experiences, their nature and value, which we have provided for the children.

A group of children from a children's home coming near to the end of two weeks' holiday at a seaside resort, had had a great deal of fun but had apparently learned little. They knew nothing of tides, how the sand came to be there or even why they had been instructed not to drink water from the sea. One child, aged 8, asked me in all seriousness, 'Where is the plug?' The inference I think is fairly obvious here. If the child is to benefit from the many experiences he has, these experiences must have point, they must be directed and focused and above all they must be preceded, accompanied and followed by questioning, discussion and the giving of new words and new shades of meaning of words already known. It is only as experience is examined through language that it can be retained and used to understand future experiences.

The child is constantly undergoing a variety of experiences in his life outside school and these will be helpful to him and can often be made use of in the classroom situation. A special importance however must be placed upon the structured experience given by the school, for this will be common to a number of children and can often be planned in advance by the teacher. Trips outside school should be frequent. I am not thinking here of the annual occasion when the whole school closes down for a visit to the zoo, the seaside or some historic town, but rather of the type of visit made by a single class which may take no more than an hour. A trip to the local church, a factory, a building site or a bus station can all become exciting bases for work and discussion when the child is helped to observe the interesting factors present. The nature walk, the observation of traffic or even people from the school playground can all be structured into pleasing projects. What we cannot go out to see we can often bring into the classroom—a corner for pets, a nature table, collections of shapes of minerals of varying weights and textures, of relics from the past—the list could be endless. Some experiences would be too time consuming at first hand or too distant for travel but these may be presented second-hand in just as interesting a fashion through the media of radio, television, pictures, films, filmstrips and slides or simply by teacher description. The sounds of the child's own environment can be collected on tape and by careful editing can be formed into interesting sequences that give new point and excitement to the familiar and commonplace. Children need to feel involved in the experiences in order to benefit fully from them and so a special place must be given to things they can do. As a child makes a model, paints a picture, plays in the sand tray or measures out an area of the playground he is as much involved in real experience as if he were to be allowed to take the wheel in a racing car.

There must also be a place for constructional toys, puppetry and free drama for these all help the child to make use of language in improving his imaginative and creative powers. Children should be fully involved in the day to day organization of their work and allowed to discuss naturally matters of organization and improvement of class facilities. They should also be personally involved in the design and leadership of such items as the school's act of corporate worship and such occasions as open days.

All these things will bring interest and enthusiasm to their daily work, will provide talking points and stimulate the natural curiosity of the children. In all this however the teacher is the representative of the adult world, the guide and director, who provides the standard of attainment towards which the children are to strive. It will be necessary therefore for the teacher to be more than involved, interested and enthusiastic in all the work with the children, she must also set the standard in linguistic excellence. The quality of the teacher's speech in width of vocabulary and sensitivity to the use of words, grammatical constructions and in its tonal variety will be reflected in the speech of the children.

Listening and language development

We have set the scene wherein the child will be stimulated by a rich experience to communicate with his fellows and also be provided with opportunities for free and structured discussion. The child however will need new words and new expressions in order to classify his experience and these he will gain by listening to the speech of others. The art of listening is more than simply giving ear to what someone else is saying. We have all met children who, having heard every word of a direction given take no action, for the instructions have simply not registered in the mind. Again we know how a simple fact can be distorted in the hands of the 'gossip'. Good listening therefore consists in the ability to understand what is said, to interpret the usage of words, phrases and intonation so that both content and intention of what is related is appreciated.

Listening is every bit as important to a successful discussion or conversation as is speaking and though we want children to speak freely, for it is only as the young child expresses his thoughts that he crystallizes his experience, it is equally valuable that he should be taught how to listen. In his school career as a whole the child probably spends 50 per cent of his time in listening, and in his leisure time this percentage is probably increased. Concentration in listening is usually easier, especially for the young child, if the sound is accompanied by some visual presentation, so the use of films and television have a special place here.

Most young children enjoy hearing the teacher read a story. In order to gain full enjoyment from this, the story must be carefully chosen for its appeal to the particular group of children to whom it is being presented. It will be helpful if the teacher can create a dramatic atmosphere by her vocal intonation and expression, for often the meaning is more clearly recognized by the child through the manner in which the words are enunciated than it would be if related in a less dramatic way.

For the child who has some difficulty in listening, special recordings can be made of sounds and speech on tape which he can be tested on later. Groups of children can play games wherein one child in turn gives directions which the others then follow; e.g. 'Touch the wall', 'Jump like a rabbit'.

Occasionally the teacher may wish the children to learn certain new words. These can be frequently repeated within the context of a story or drawn from the children by a series of questions.

e.g. Children are shown a picture of a bus.

Words for study	Questions
front	Where is the engine of the bus?
	Which is the front of the bus?
	Who sits at the front of the bus?
round	How many wheels has the bus?
	What are the wheels for?
	What shape are the wheels?
	Why are they round?
	Tell me some other things that are round.
driver	How does the driver steer the bus?
	What does the driver use his feet for?
	Where is the driver sitting?

Reading and language development
We have noted the many ways in which language development aids growth in reading ability and that in the early stages of reading all words which the child is asked to read should already be present in his speech vocabulary. It may not be quite so obvious that reading itself is of value to language development as a whole.

From the very beginning the child gains from his reading book, knowledge of how words can be used from the points of view of meaning and sentence construction. At a later stage he will be able to learn new words and appreciate their meaning as he meets them in the context of his reader. Reading also gives knowledge which can later form the basis of conversation or be the starting point of some imaginative project. Again it provides for a wider sphere of second-hand experience and brings help to the activity of classification and generalization from past experience. Lastly reading, in that punctuation has been supplied, helps many children to appreciate more the importance of pause and emphasis in speech.

Writing and language development
Written work has a special appeal as children feel its increased permanency in comparison to speech and also get a greater feeling of creative achievement when they can repeatedly turn to a piece of work they themselves have written.

Writing also draws attention to the structure of the language, the sound value of letters in words, the construction of phrases and sentences. As the child writes, the steadier pace allows greater time for contemplation and a more effective method of expressing a particular thought than does speech.

Listening and reading
Listening helps the child to relate the sound and the visual symbol by which it is represented in print and therefore is an aid to word recognition. It directs attention to words which have common sounds and helps the child appreciate the necessity of variations in vocal expression.

The child who has heard a story or part of it read by the teacher, who has perhaps taken part in a dramatization of it will be highly motivated to read the story for himself and make much more intelligent use of the context when he meets a hitherto unknown word. Some teachers record early reading texts on tape and the child can follow the words in the book as he listens to the tape or read it in unison with the teacher's voice. The Language Master uses the principle of listening and reading admirably and can be very useful in introducing the child to new words and sentences in preparation perhaps for a new and more difficult reading text.

Writing and reading
In the early stages of reading, writing and reading will be part of the same activity. The child will want to provide a caption to his pictures and models just as the teacher does to hers and he should be

encouraged to do so. As the child writes, so he is reading and he will come back to the picture over and over again and proudly read the caption. This activity will be extended until the child is writing his own little books about things which are vital to him at the moment and cooperating with others in recording a joint experience.

The teaching of handwriting appears to be rather out of fashion as far as most teachers are concerned and to me this is a matter for regret. Many children are slow to turn to creative writing simply because they lack the necessary tools. Moreover an untrained hand usually makes large numbers of unnecessary movements and is uneconomical in the use of the child's time. I would argue that for the value gained for the reading process the child should be helped to form his letters in an expert manner as early in his school life as possible. Writing is undoubtedly the best training for left/right orientation in reading and I have often noted that a short course in letter formation helps the child who tends to reverse or invert letters. Written work also aids word recognition in that it draws attention to the letter patterns which form the word and of the contribution of the individual letter to the whole word.

Many children find difficulty in reading a word when it is located in a new context or placed on its own despite the fact that they have no hesitation when they meet the word in their reader. There are many possible reasons for this, but writing helps to overcome two of them, namely seeing the word in a slightly different type of print and secondly giving practice in recognition of the word in a new setting, thus gaining consolidation of learning which is taking place. Thus writing is of real help to the child in helping him to build a sight vocabulary.

Fernald believed that many children gained great help in word recognition from writing—so much so that she based a whole series of remedial techniques upon writing with a good deal of success.

Finally the child's attempts at creative writing will reveal to what extent he has gained mastery of the vocabulary of his reader and will also be helpful in providing clues to the child's interests and emotional needs.

Looking, thinking and reading
The definition of reading proposed early in this book suggested that reading was a thinking and reacting process. On entry to school the young child is capable of considerable powers of thinking and

these must be harnessed early to produce the effective reader. First impressions and attitudes are often the strongest and therefore the early stages of reading must have a balance between the mastery of the more mechanical aspects of word recognition and the pursuit of thinking in relation to content. Many of the thinking activities we wish to develop later in dealing with print can be prepared for by using picture books. Children can discuss situational pictures stimulated by questions posed by the teacher. For example, a picture of a monkey leaping from one tree to another with a falling coconut poised above his head might be used in the following way:

1. Children name the objects in the picture.
2. They describe what is happening.
3. What will happen?
   (i) Will the coconut hit the monkey?
   (ii) What might happen if it does?
4. Why did the coconut fall?

A further strategy is to cut up into groups of three or four pictures a good quality story presented in comic strip form. The children can be presented with each group in turn. The teacher will then ask 'What might happen? Why do you think this will happen? What is there in the picture which tells you this might happen?'

If the story is well chosen the children will be placed in a valid problem-solving situation and will gain the habit of looking at pictures and reading with a questioning and thoughtful attitude, reviewing all the information presented not a little at a time but every section in turn in relation to the whole.

Encouraging the development of visual and auditory skills
Experiences, interest and enthusiasm will be gained for the reading process from our general work in the language arts, but we must be sure that the child also has the basic tools for the job. We will take care therefore to gain a knowledge of the child's ability to discriminate the fine differences in symbol and sound that are present in our language. Armed with a knowledge of the child's maturity in discrimination, perception and memory the teacher can then devise activities which are helpful to his progress. Most modern reading schemes have books of 'pre-reading' material consisting of pictures for discussion, observation and completion exercises, recognition of similarities and differences and orientation exercises. For some children these may be sufficient in number to bring the

child to the stage where he can read his first 'real' book. For the child who needs further work some of the activities below may be found helpful. It has been mentioned earlier that such activities will be helpful to children when they are making headway in the reading scheme and to this end some suggestions are included for work at a rather higher level.

Visual perception

1. The completion of jigsaw puzzles is an enjoyable activity for many children and requires considerable skill in matching and the making of a whole from a number of parts. Similar matching activities can be gained from games using snap cards or dominoes—for the very young children the 'Noddy' pictures dominoes will arouse enthusiasm.

2. Colouring outline drawings, tracing and drawing with templates and the joining together of dots to form pictures are helpful for motor control as well as visual discrimination.

3. Picture interpretation. When reading a book the child can sometimes gain the vital clue to an unknown word by reference to the illustration. So often however children seem to miss the point of the picture and thus cannot use this type of aid. The activity of picture observation and interpretation trains the child to look at things and relate two dimensional drawings to his experience of real things. The activity is also a part of language growth and experience and so the same pictures could be used for oral composition.

4. Matching exercises. These consist of sets of pictures in twos. The child is given a pile of these and has to arrange them in identical pairs. At a later stage this becomes a true reading activity as the child matches letter to letter, word to word and word to picture. The gummed picture stamps from Philip and Tacey are most helpful here.

5. The above activity can be made a little more advanced in a workbook format by selecting identical pictures, shapes or words from groups of similar items.

△	○	□	▽	◇	△
big	bag	dig	bog	big	beg

6. Posting activities. The sorting of shapes, pictures, letters and words into boxes where the teacher can check the child's work at a glance can be most helpful. This activity can be further extended by requesting the child to sort pictures or words into groups under headings such as food, clothing, toys etc.

7. For the children whose discrimination is still immature the party game of guessing objects which have been removed from a group can be helpful.

8. Crossing out letters on simple letter sheets e.g. cross out the 'b's' in the following list: a b e f b b c d b a d b

Left/right orientation

This skill is not normally learned naturally and many children will come to school needing to undertake specific work in this skill before making a successful attempt at reading the printed word.

1. The reading of comics, though perhaps questionable training from the point of view of literary appreciation, is helpful to orientation in that the pictures as well as the text are arranged in a left to right sequence.

2. The child will enjoy sorting action pictures into a left right sequence showing the various stages in one complete action. A useful source of such materials is the wealth of sporting annuals which are provided for children. The same activity can also be worked out with a series of pictures which tell a story. The Remedial Supply Company Ltd, have published material for this activity.

3. Simple mazes.

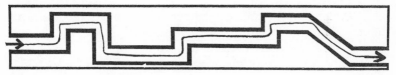

4. Tracing and colouring letters or using letter templates and then drawing an appropriate illustration.

5. Written work is undoubtedly a very great help in achieving efficiency in left/right orientation. However, merely allowing the child to write is not the answer, for before maximum value can be gained from the activity the child must construct his letter in a helpful manner. If this is done not only letter recognition will be improved, but the child will be able to write with greater economy and eventually greater speed. Observing children write who have been given little or no training in letter formation, I have discovered that they tend to make their pencil travel much farther than is necessary and a vast number fall into the habit of constructing letters in the reverse direction. The child who starts both the 'b' and the 'd' by producing the upright stroke first finds his writing a hindrance rather than a help to the recognition of the differences between these two letters.

6. All the normal activities associated with letter and word recognition and phonic work will be helpful, especially where they bring a second sense into play so that there is a visual/touch relationship or a visual/sound relationship. Thus sorting and posting of letters and words and the making of words from individual letters cut from cards will prove helpful.

Visual memory

Again memorization of words will always be helped if they are presented through a number of senses, thus sight, touch and hearing combined will give the best chance of successful retention.

1. Completion of drawings of common objects which have some parts missing.
2. Drawing simple geometric figures after a brief exposure of the figure. This can also be done with words.
3. Tracing and writing letters and words.
4. Writing words from memory e.g. the use of sentences with a missing word.

Auditory discrimination

1. The use of percussion and musical instruments.
2. Listening for sounds and later sounds within sounds e.g. a bicycle bell being rung during a peal of church bells. Later this can be undertaken by listening for particular letter sounds in various positions within words. A whole series of such exercises could be prepared with the use of a tape recorder.
3. The game of 'I spy'.

4. Singing games and nursery rhymes.
5. Rhyming words.
6. Obeying oral instructions.
7. The teaching of the letter sounds of the alphabet.

Although the foregoing skills and abilities have been considered under separate headings it must not be thought that they are entirely independent activities. For example any printed word that is perceived visually will also bring into operation previous language experience and visual and auditory memory. It would be wrong therefore, to subject the child to long courses of training in any one particular skill and the activities suggested are merely guides to enable the teacher to check that the instruction is giving to each child the background which is essential to his progress. It will readily be seen that such a width of activities includes work in all areas of the curriculum and this must be so, for all our work involves communication and reading is one important part of this all pervading art.

Auditory-visual integration
It has already been noted that progress in the early stages of reading is influenced by the extent to which children are able to relate the spatial sequencing of written language to the temporal sequencing of spoken language. Many of the activities which have been mentioned above help to develop this ability but some children may need extra help. The use of percussion instruments and recorders in conjunction with some type of musical notation is not only a natural and enjoyable part of normal school work, valid for its own sake, but can be most successful in developing auditory-visual integration.

This example illustrates well a most important primary consideration in reading teaching, namely that when the teacher understands the nature of the learning task for the child, a natural and enjoyable activity can usually become a vehicle for the learning. All too often many areas of the curriculum which could give great help to reading growth have not been allowed to provide such help and as a result the children have transferred their boredom with drills and devised activities to the whole area of reading. They have mastered the skills but have not found joy or profit in reading. Keith Gardner has expressed this succinctly in a criticism of some approaches to remedial teaching which he suggested simply produced 'more statistically respectable non-readers'.

Involving the parents

Lady Plowden recently urged that teachers should take parents much more into their confidence concerning the aims of school and the work their children are doing. Parents in general have never before shown more interest in the educational growth of their children than they do today. Teachers could, I feel, meet parents more frequently and more freely in school. Some few parents seem reluctant to enter the school and the teacher should therefore endeavour to visit the home. The parental interest is often there if only we cultivate it and we cannot expect them to grow in understanding of our work in school unless we give them every opportunity to develop this understanding.

From the point of view of reading there is so much that the parent can do to help and indeed many parents are already involved in doing this. How much more successful this would be if we could instruct the parents in the provision of a helpful educational atmosphere before the child reaches school. Again how much more effective would the reading undertaken at home be in the child's total reading growth if parents were advised on how to hear their children read and how to provide for a wide range of language and literary experiences.

In summary therefore the early weeks of a child's life in school are seen as a time for assessment of the child's development. Armed with a full knowledge of the child the teacher will provide a full programme of experience which will complement past experience and where necessary compensate for a lack of experience due to poor environmental conditions. In the stimulating atmosphere provided the child will feel the need for wider communication and speech, listening and thinking will improve in range and quality. The children will soon experience the desire to make their communication more permanent by writing it down and class and individual books composed by the children will be created and these will form the core of early work in reading. Most young children seem to have a stronger desire to write than they do to read and thus this approach fits in with their development. The child having gained success from reading his own written work, will soon show a desire to read more widely.

Further reading

GODDARD, N. L. (1962) *Reading in Modern Infant Classes* ULP

GOODACRE, E. J. (1971) *Children and Learning to Read* Routledge and
Kegan Paul

HUGHES, J. M. (1971) *Aids to Reading* Evans

ROBERTS, G. R. (1969) *Reading in Primary Schools* Routledge and
Kegan Paul

STAUFFER, R. G. (1970) *Learning to Read as a Thinking Process* Harper
and Row

CHAPTER 10

Reading schemes and their usage

The reading scheme has been strongly criticized in recent years as being an unnatural and uninteresting way of taking a child through the early stages of reading. Despite this criticism the majority of teachers in infant schools continue to make use of one or more such schemes and publishers continue to produce them.

A reading scheme can be helpful to the teacher and child in the following ways:

1. It provides a framework for controlled growth of vocabulary and word recognition skills.
2. The repetition of words helps the children to memorize them.
3. Progress through the scheme is evidence of success to the child and of speed of progress and competence to the teacher.
4. The child gains confidence through the security afforded by a controlled vocabulary.

The reading scheme can however have the following weaknesses or disadvantages, especially if only one such scheme is available for the child to use.

1. The content may be irrelevant to the interests of the individual child.
2. The language employed in the early books is often stilted and the vocabulary developed not very helpful when reading other books.
3. Often the child is continually challenged to learn new words and new sentence patterns. This can detract from thoughtful consideration of the content, limit the achievement of varied reading speeds at a later date and help form the habit of 'barking at print'.
4. No one scheme provides the range of language and reading experience needed to make the child a truly independent reader.

The important considerations at the present time are to select and use carefully good materials rather than expect a reading scheme, of itself, to teach the child to read.

Attributes of a good reading scheme

1. The content should be of interest to the children, providing lively stories which are based in the type of experiences which are common to the majority of young children.

2. The vocabulary used in the early stages should be within the language experience of the children.

3. The introduction of new words must be carefully controlled and sufficient repetition of these words should be included to ensure their memorization by the average child.

4. The books should be attractive to the child, and the illustrations clear and helpful to the reading of the text.

5. The print should be clear and simple and its size related to the visual acuity of the age of the child for which the book is designed.

6. The books should not be so lengthy that the child feels it a marathon task to read to the end.

7. The books should encourage reading with understanding, sequential thought and the steady formulation of new concepts.

8. Starting with simple grammatical constructions, a growth in sentence complexity should be evident. This simple beginning must not however lead to meaningless and stilted text.

9. As the scheme progresses so should the variation in type of story and width of interest grow.

10. The scheme should include a variety of activities, workbooks and games in addition to the readers.

In purchasing a reading scheme the head teacher and staff of the school will need to assess carefully the materials within it and the methods advocated by the author in the accompanying manual. It is probable that the final decision will be to buy more than one scheme and in this case it is suggested that schemes which differ in their approach and yet can be complementary to each other should be considered. A central scheme based upon mixed methods could be aligned with a predominantly phonic and/or sentence approach. In this way a wide range of parallel work in reading will be available together with the ability to provide for the individual abilities and interests exhibited by the children. Further the school will have provided for the growth of all facets of reading skill.

When is a child ready to use a reading scheme?

There can really be no hard and fast set of rules which will answer this question and in the final analysis the teacher will have to make this decision for each individual child, partly from a knowledge of the child's maturity and ability and partly, I am afraid, in hope and faith. Failures should be few however if the teacher has prepared the ground carefully. There are children who never show any real enthusiasm, interest or ability in reading until they are given a book and told to read it. They then surprise everyone, not least themselves, by making a real success of the activity and creating a new and valued addition to their daily life. In order to guard against failure to the best of our ability the following list of attributes and attainments is given to guide the teacher when making the decision.

1. The child should want to read books.
2. He should be capable of reasonable periods of concentration.
3. He should have a fairly wide spoken vocabulary and be capable of expressing his own thoughts in speech in a consecutive manner.
4. He should be mature in visual and auditory discrimination.
5. He should have some attainment in letter and word recognition.
6. He should be able to interpret simple pictures.
7. He should have proved by his use of picture books and other materials that he can treat books in a respectful manner.

It is in fact a much simpler matter to give a decision upon when a child is ready to read the first book in a reading scheme than it is to say whether he is ready for the scheme as a whole, but it must also be stressed that the future hoped for progress must be taken into account. Unless this is done the child, having made a good start may quickly come to a standstill for the necessary interest in and enthusiasm for reading may not have been present. To read the first book of a reading scheme the child must know the meanings of all the words in that book and be able to recognize them on sight. If this precaution is taken success is assured. Some teachers feeling that the content of the early books in the reading scheme is not sufficiently meaningful, endeavour to teach all the words in the early books and commence use of the scheme at a later book. Whilst in sympathy with their opinions I feel it worthwhile to allow the child the opportunity of reading these early books, for the feeling of success gained and the training in the approach to the reading book which is given. Again as the number of words used in the later books becomes greater it is increasingly difficult to devise activities which will ensure the child's retention of so many words and yet at the same time retain their interest and enthusiasm.

Activities to precede the introduction of a reading scheme
A very heavy learning load is placed upon the child who is expected to begin reading the first primer in a reading scheme without

extensive preparation. The first experiences with books may set up life-long attitudes towards reading so the teacher must take every care to legislate for success.

A period of time where the child is given considerable support in his reading usually proves helpful. This support can be achieved by the use of a story method approach where the teacher reads a short but engaging story and the child reads a summary of this story afterwards. An even more foolproof approach is to record the text of simple caption books along with a chatty discussion of the illustrations and let the child read the text together with the tape. An excellent series for this purpose are the Pre-Reading Books produced by the Remedial Supply Company.

The child needs a strong interest in the use of language if interest in books is to be maintained. He needs to feel at the beginning that 'reading is talk written down' and that there are distinct advantages in putting speech into a more permanent form. This can be achieved by encouraging children to talk and write about their own experiences.

The following suggestions are possible ways of introducing the child to a reading scheme and giving him support during his progress through the first few books. No one child is likely to need to use them all, and some of the more recent reading schemes give greater opportunities for relating the reading book to the experiences which the child has in real life or which can be worked out in the classroom.

1. Make full use of any pre-reading material which is provided by the author of the reading scheme.

2. Tell stories which introduce characters from the reading scheme. Short stories using folk tales and nursery rhymes can be used as the basis for pictures and small booklets which incorporate the use of the vocabulary of the reader.

3. Children paint portraits of the characters which are then labelled and displayed.

4. Dramatization of simple stories, involving characters from the reading scheme. Here name labels can be attached to children to show which characters they are playing. Scenery of a makeshift nature can also be supplied and labelled.

5. Miming games to gain mastery of action words.

6. Establish a reading corner for materials, books, pictures and models relative to the reading scheme.

7. The use of flash cards, word and picture and sentence and picture matching cards.

8. The arrangement of a number of words into a sentence which explains a given illustration.

9. The use of lotto, dominoes and snap cards using words from the scheme. Lotto is particularly good for teaching words such as 'the', 'who', 'there' etc. which appear with such frequency yet are much more difficult to give practice in, than are nouns, verbs and adjectives.

10. Items 2 and 4 above could well be combined and photographed and the prints captioned for reading practice or turned into filmstrips for group work.

11. The use of the Language Master to teach words and sentences to individuals.

12. Films or filmstrips of the main events of the book accompanied by children's reading of the actual text. In this way a group of children can see the action performed and read the text as it is spoken by a child from a more advanced group or previous year possibly recorded on tape.

13. Workbook activities incorporating drawing, colouring, missing word exercises and choice questions relative to the text. The example given below is taken from some work given as an introduction to Tansley's *Racing to Read* scheme. This series of books is recommended for use with retarded children in the junior school but similar activities could equally well be designed for any introductory reader.

Put the right colour in these squares

red [ ] blue [ ] green [ ]

This is my house.

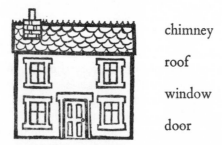

chimney

roof

window

door

Ask the child to colour the house using the three colours mentioned —write the colours on the picture and draw arrows from the words to the parts of the picture they describe.

Draw and colour pictures in these boxes

A red chimney	A blue door
A red roof	A blue window
A green door	A green window

Underline the right sentence

This is a roof
This is a window
This is a door

This is a roof
This is a chimney
This is a door

It is a door
It is a chimney
It is a window

It is a roof

It is a door

It is a window

Draw and colour a picture of a house.
Put in: A red roof
             A red chimney
             A blue door
             A blue window
             A green tree

Draw a picture of a red roof

1. The roof is....................... .
2. My house has a....................... .
3. The roof of...................house is red.

Draw a picture of a red chimney

4. This is a................... .
5. It is a...................chimney.
6. The chimney of my house.............red.

Draw a red chimney on a roof

7. My house has a red...................and................... .

Draw a blue door

8. This...................is blue.
9. My...................has a door.
10. The door of my house is................... .

Look at the picture of the house   **Yes or no**

11. Is the roof red?   ....
12. Is the door green?   ....

13. Is the chimney red? ....

14. Is the door blue? ....

15. Is the roof green? ....

14. Teach letter recognition and the sounds of letters through games and the commencement of a picture dictionary.

The foregoing activities though helpful should be used alongside the continuing provision of experiences and the development of all language arts. There should therefore be no real division between the two types of activities but the more limited and directly applied techniques described above should be welded into the continuing language experience.

Using the reading scheme

All too frequently schools, having laid out a large section of their finance upon a reading scheme, become its captive. It must be stressed that on every occasion that a child nears the end of a book, his next book should be selected as a result of a review of his needs and a reassessment of the immediate, as against the long term aims of the child's reading programme. It does not follow because a child has successfully completed Book 3 of the reading scheme that he should automatically move on to Book 4. It may be that he is in need of further practice at the same level, or that to keep up successful progress he needs to have a period of reading a more phonically based text. Again it may be felt that the stories of another book at the appropriate standard are more related to the child's needs and immediate interests. The slow child may need considerable practice at the same level before proceeding to more advanced work whilst the bright child might be held back by insisting that he reads each book in the scheme in succession. The reading scheme should therefore be our servant and not our master. The necessary flexibility can be achieved by having all our books listed according to type of approach, attainment level and comparable vocabulary. A specimen plan of such an aid is briefly set out together with appropriate activities opposite. Obviously any one class would have a wide range of supplementary material which would also be included in the list. Here only the main schemes are listed.

Parallel schemes

A plan modelled on that given overleaf is admirable for selecting

Reading Stage	Pre-Reading	5·0 to 5·3	5·4 to 5·6	5·7 to 5·9	5·10 to 6·0	6·1 to 6·3	6·4 to 6·6	6·7 to 6·9
Happy Trio Readers	We read pictures / We read more pictures / Before we read / The Big Book	We look and see	We work and play	We come and go	Guess who?	Fun with Dick and Jane Part 1	Fun with Dick and Jane Part 2	Our new friends Part 1
McKee Readers	Getting Ready	Book 1		Book 2	Platform Readers A Series	Book 3	Platform Readers B Series	Book 4
Gay Way Readers				Red Book	Red Stories	Green Book	Green Stories	Blue Book
General activities	Picture to Picture Matching / Picture and Word Matching / Word to Word Matching / Flash card work					Comprehension work / Making own readers		
	Single letter sounds / Letter tracing and letter making in plasticine / Posting letters / Lexicon / Key Words / Lotto			Analysis and synthesis of three letter regular words				

books which require a roughly equivalent reading attainment, for successful reading. Most children will at some stage require more practice at a particular stage in their development than is supplied within the limits of a single scheme. It is also most necessary that they should at quite an early stage in reading have acquaintance with the slightly different style, the variation in vocabulary and the different interests of another author.

A few years ago McDonald produced a plan whereby a number of introductory readers from our established reading schemes were ranked for the minimum introduction of new' words. Some 11 books were listed, with a total vocabulary of 164 words and an average number of new words per book of 15. On the surface this seems admirable for the achievement of individual success but if employed would present many difficulties. Sixteen per cent of the new words were the names of people and pets and this would lead to confusion in the child's mind. The books at this stage have little story content and therefore it would probably be difficult to maintain interest. Again when the child had read all these books his total readiness for the next stage of the single reading scheme is perhaps improved by extensive practice but the width of vocabulary gained is not extremely helpful. It would seem better therefore to give the extensive practice necessary to memorize the words introduced in the early books of a scheme through apparatus, games and work-books. It will readily be seen that the system of parallel books though valuable can be over used. The value of the idea lies in the following features.

1. It gives extra practice at an equivalent attainment level for the child who needs this.
2. It allows for work in phonics and comprehension to continue at the same level as the work in the reader.
3. It provides for a variety of interests among children.
4. It gives practice in a wider vocabulary and varying literary styles.
5. It is most helpful to the teacher in the organization of her available reading materials.

A great deal of confusion and uneconomic use of a reading scheme can arise unless the teacher's guide is closely studied. In America teachers often work word for word and step by step according to the guide whereas in this country far fewer schools buy the guides than purchase the schemes and even those bought rarely seem to be read. A guide is usually invaluable in building up a picture of the author's purpose in composing the scheme and in realizing how the scheme has been constructed and the approach for which it was designed. Very often the guide contains not only information on how the author intended the scheme to be used, but also many ideas for supplementary activities. A happy medium lies somewhere between the opposite approaches of the two sets of teachers where the teacher in full knowledge of the author's views and suggestions then uses the scheme in a way which suits the children and herself. In this way the expertise and the inventiveness of both author and class teacher will be fully used.

The reading scheme is not to be looked upon as providing all the practice and activities the child needs in order to increase his reading attainment. There is no scheme sufficiently wide ranging to do this nor would it be desirable. Alongside the reading scheme or schemes the general experience work and the improvement of proficiency in speaking, listening and writing must be pursued. Skill in word recognition and comprehension will not improve at the best possible rate unless some definite instruction is given in the techniques involved. Again children and teachers alike seem to become obsessed by the idea of constant steady progress and feel that each new book should challenge the child to reach a new level in attainment. This is not a realistic view of the way in which children develop or indeed in the way reading growth takes place. It is more usual for progress to be made by a succession of spurts interspersed with periods of consolidation. Realizing this, we will endeavour to ally our use of readers and instruction to meet these needs. When the child is forging ahead he can read a number of pages to the teacher or read large portions of the book to himself and only occasional pages to the teacher. At other times it may be necessary to read a single page on any one occasion or to move to another book of the same standard. The child will not do all his reading from the book in the reading scheme that is appropriate to his attainment. He will read other books for his own pleasure or seek specific knowledge from a reference book. When a child is reading for his own pleasure in school it is helpful if this reading can be undertaken at a level of attainment which is a little below his own, for then he will be able to enjoy the story without the strain of having to deal with words he has not met before.

As attainment and fluency increase the need for the security offered by the controlled vocabulary of the reading scheme decreases. It is right therefore that most reading schemes come to an end at the approximate reading level of an average 9-year-old child. At this level a controlled vocabulary can become a restricting rather than a helpful factor. Learning to read does not however end at this level of attainment, considerable progress still needs to be made. Some children will continue to make good progress and many will make fair progress above this level simply by reading books. It is certain however that the future attainment would be higher and progress more rapid if instruction were to be maintained in some form throughout school life. This matter will be further discussed in Chapter 13.

Further reading
GARDNER, W. K. (1965) *Towards Literacy* Blackwell

MURRAY, W. (1969) *Teaching Reading* Wills and Hepworth

ROBERTS, G. R. (1969) *Reading in Primary Schools* Routledge and Kegan Paul

CHAPTER II

Beginning reading without a scheme

There has been a growing feeling among infant school teachers that the use of a reading scheme does not fit in with the other activities of the school, or that the schemes themselves are restrictive and uninteresting. There are now schools in which reading schemes are no longer used at all. In some schools the change has been highly successful, but in others something of a disaster.

The purpose of this chapter is to suggest strategies for achieving the aims for reading teaching set out at the beginning of this book, which do not employ the traditional reading scheme. All of them would extend beyond the normal boundaries of reading work and most could be used equally well alongside a reading scheme. The teacher intending to follow these suggestions must however accept from the outset that her work load will be heavier, though somewhat more stimulating, than if she were to use a reading scheme.

Systematic work

Some schools have experienced a considerable fall in standards after discarding the reading scheme because they have lacked clearly defined objectives and a programme of systematic work to achieve them. Whatever the weaknesses of reading schemes, they do provide the teacher and child with a ready-made structure aimed at the expansion of reading skill. The teacher must replace this with something which will achieve the same or superior ends. To provide such a structure does not imply a plan of instruction to be followed slavishly, but involves an analysis of the elements of the reading task which can act as a guide for general classroom policy and a diagnostic check list for the individual child. The teacher will begin such an analysis by suggesting the stage of development she feels the children should reach at the end of the period of her personal responsibility for them. The next step is to fill in the major steps that the individual child needs to take in order to progress from his present level of attainment to the new level set. In making such an analysis it immediately becomes obvious that it is quite unnecessary to devise specific skill training activities for each step. Rather it will be easier to see how such steps can be achieved through real-life, enjoyable and useful activities, many of which are not thought to be developing reading skills. The following areas will need to be considered in the infant and junior school though not all will be necessary at all stages.

1. Perceptual development.
2. Development of a knowledge of the spelling patterns of English.
3. Growth of understanding of word meanings.
4. Extension of knowledge of sentence patterns.
5. Development of the ability to read with understanding.
6. The expansion of the uses of and purposes in reading.
7. Development of thinking and reacting to the printed page.

The teaching approach recommended here is that the child is presented with situations involving real-life problems and activities and the need to complete them. The children will see the need for specific skills and varied stimulating materials will be made available for the child to select in order to learn the skill. The teacher too, in working together with the children, will be able to provide teaching which develops the skills needed. For example, the young child may not be able to distinguish between 'b' and 'd'. The child can have great fun fitting ball bearings into an outline frame, similar to the toy puzzles commercially available. A picture of a familiar object beginning with the letter should be shown in the background.

It is possible to construct letters from glass tubes which fill with a coloured liquid in the direction that the letter should be written when a tap is turned under the picture of a common object which starts with that letter.

An older child may pick up a reference book knowing that it contains information he wants access to but finds the vocabulary beyond him. This presents the teacher with an ideal opportunity to become involved with the child, helping him to solve this language puzzle by leading him to examine picture, context, configuration probability and phonic clues until all the elements of the puzzle fall into place.

Modules of materials can be built up under each of the headings 1-7 above. The teacher will of course need to cater for a variety of tastes in the reading matter, including the real-life, information books, fantasy stories and humour, poetry, prose and song. In building such modules it will be necessary to grade for difficulty of books involved. This can be done with a readability formula or older children can grade the books themselves using cloze procedure. (See J. GILLILAND (1972) *Readability* ULP for further help here.) When grading has taken place some system of signalling the reading level to the children such as the use of coloured stars will be most helpful.

Some publishers particularly in America have realized the restrictions of the reading scheme and have produced modules of materials which are carefully matched for reading level at each stage. Often however they show too great a concern for mechanical skills and pay insufficient attention to variety in the content. As a result they are often little more than greatly extended reading schemes. In some ways, the greater variety of a range of materials of this type compiled by the teacher is preferable even though the reading levels and vocabulary employed may not be perfectly matched.

Making a start
One of the major difficulties of dispensing with a reading scheme is the building of a core vocabulary from which the child can work towards increasing independence. Two possibilities here, the use of the story method and reading in conjunction with a tape recorder, have already been discussed. Of great value too will be the child's own personal vocabulary which he wants to record as captions to pictures, models and graphs. If the teacher provides sufficient stimulus, the children will provide the language. Then the teacher must select those words which need explanation, those words which provide source material for making generalizations about spelling patterns, and those sentences and phrases which need careful examination when intonation and pause may change their meaning.

Reading-thinking activities
Individual work is always a necessary feature of reading teaching especially in the early stage of reading development. It does unfortunately tend to isolate children and therefore opportunities must be provided for informal discussion among the children concerning the material they have read and the written work they have produced. This leads to a livelier interpretation of the material, the exercise of thinking critically about what has been read and a higher standard of communication in written work produced.

There is much to be gained from more formal group work throughout school life for the discussion of material read. This can be achieved in a variety of ways but two particular examples are described below:

1. A small group of children read a story silently in serial form. After reading each section they discuss with their teacher and each other how the story might continue. The teacher will be at pains to ensure, by discreet questioning, that imagination is not allowed to run riot. Every possible idea must be supported by a reason and evidence quoted from the section read. Each time a further episode is read the children review and modify the previous suggestions given. Apart from encouraging anticipation, the reading of material with insight and a questioning attitude on the part of the children, the teacher will be able to help extend understanding of words and sentence patterns and note any weaknesses in the ability to understand the meaning expressed.

2. Cloze procedure, though developed as a device for measuring readability, can be a most useful teaching device. One group of children can prepare material for another by counting out say every tenth word and covering it with masking tape. The children try first to fill all the spaces individually. Having done this they come together in a group and compare their answers, discussing the ones on which they do not agree. In this discussion they will have to explain why they reached the conclusion they did and this encourages reading with anticipation and a questioning attitude. Finally agreed responses are compared with the author's original word. Where differences occur, they may be synonyms and children can reflect on the appropriateness of their word compared with the author's. This in itself leads to an appreciation of style. Where the word the children found was incorrect they have to review whether they asked the right questions in order to fill the space, whether they understood the idea being expressed and whether they had made use of all the contextual clues available.

This particular exercise needs careful preparatory work over a period of time and the following steps prove helpful.

a. Missing words in single sentences with a list of words to select from.

b. As above, but the initial letter of the missing word given with the number of letters in the word shown.

c. Short passages with an odd word omitted here and there with a variety of clues—number of letters, a first or final letter or a distinctive group of letters, e.g. 'tion' or 'ough'.

Real-life activities

Much of the work of schools is too far removed from the children's everyday life and experience. Even relatively informal activities such as projects are often carried out at the suggestion of the teacher without any foundation in the real interests and needs of the children. They quickly lose interest and the teacher is unable to make use of the project for sustaining growth and development in reading.

Projects should arise from the expressed thoughts of the children and should be guided by the teacher in such a way that they examine and create language which is important to their immediate needs. Through this they will come to appreciate the importance of language and reading and will be much more strongly motivated to carry out work in the areas of skill development which the teacher must continually provide as she sees the opportunity arise. Learning based on experience is valuable at all stages of school life in developing in children an awareness of their society and environment but the teacher must be careful to take advantage of the opportunities for skill development as they occur.

CHAPTER 12

Aids to word recognition

Fluency and intelligent reading of the printed word can only be fully achieved if the child can raise his ability in word recognition to the stage of an almost automatic response. When this has been achieved all the child's energies can be directed towards the expression and interpretation of the material read. If the child is to reach this goal it will be necessary to give him instruction and practice in the following areas.

1. *Key words*
In the early stages of reading the most used words of the language must be quickly mastered for they are essential for any adequate use of context as a means of word recognition. Perhaps the best list at this particular stage is that produced by McNally and Murray (1962) which is sectioned into groups according to the frequency with which the words occur. These words appear so often in children's books but experience shows that they are not so easily committed to memory, probably due to the fact that young children find help in the more concrete parts of speech, nouns, adjectives and verbs, which do not occur so frequently. The most used words are mainly articles, prepositions, conjunctions and pronouns. The child is obviously more highly motivated to read the word 'ice cream' than the word 'who'.

2. *Phonic work*
Some skill in the analysis of a word into its component sounds and the blending of these sounds into whole words is essential to progress from two major standpoints. Firstly, the child is limited in his early reading to the number of whole words he can commit to memory in any given period. Given a knowledge of sound symbol relationship and some elementary technique for the blending of sounds his reading vocabulary will be able to expand at a more speedy rate.

Secondly, at all stages the child and indeed the adult will meet words which are unfamiliar and the use of phonic knowledge together with the context will present the most successful means of recognition.

3. The use of context

The use of context as a means of word recognition assumes skill in comprehending the passage. The ability to comprehend, in its turn, demands a knowledge of word meanings. Thus in order to help the child to make use of context to discover the unknown word we will need to provide instruction in word study and comprehension skills.

Having urged the necessity of giving instruction in the above areas it must be stressed that such instruction will only be successful if the following safeguards are observed.

1. Such instruction should correlate with and be helpful to general work in the language arts and to the reading in which the child is currently engaged. It should never be given to the exclusion or overshadowing of these activities. For most children instruction and activities in these associated skills will take up only a minority of the time available for language work and will generally be more essential for the poor reader than the child who is making very good progress.

2. The child must understand what he is being asked to do and the skills learned should be practised when reading. The teacher will need to keep a watchful eye upon this factor during the sessions when the child reads to her.

3. Such instruction and activities will only be used in the light of a knowledge of the individual child's needs. In this way the child will not be submitted to the boredom of undertaking activity in a skill which he has already fully mastered nor yet be given work which is beyond his capabilities.

4. When instruction is given to a class or group of children, the teacher must ensure that all those participating not only need the instruction but all benefit from it. Often in group work some children learn the skill quickly and overshadow the rest of the group by answering all the questions. The teacher must never be led into thinking that all members of a group will have gained equal mastery of the skill involved. It will be necessary therefore to have an adequate means of assessing the proficiency in the activity for each individual child.

5. A good deal of work in the field of word recognition can be undertaken, after a brief introduction, by the use of apparatus, games and workbooks. The use of these aids is helpful in allowing the teacher more time to concentrate upon the needs of individual children. Such activities however bring their own peculiar difficulties and the teacher must ensure that when she requires children to work with apparatus the following conditions have been satisfied.

a. The purpose of the activity is clearly understood by both teacher and child.

b. It is the best available means of achieving the desired aim.

c. All children taking part need the practice involved and can benefit from it.

d. Apparatus is always more valuable if self corrective. If this is not possible the teacher must make sure that the errors made by individual children are given speedy attention.

e. All children concerned are actively employed.

f. Apparatus of this type is best restricted to specific use and not made available to the children in free choice activity lessons.

The teaching of key words

1. Use them as frequently as possible in captions to pictures, labels and directions.

> e.g. The traditional label 'cupboard' could be replaced by:-
> This is a cupboard.
> Here is a cupboard.
> The cupboard has two doors.
> We keep pens in the cupboard. etc.

In addition a pocket could be placed beside the sentences containing sentence cards for matching work and word cards from which the sentences can be recreated.

2. Let all the children have a list of such words which they can consult when writing.

3. Some key words, but by no means all, can be included in early phonic work.

4. The use of missing word exercises.

5. Draw the attention of children to pairs of words in the list. These can if desired be made the subject of a game based on happy families or rummy. Writing of the words should not be ignored. Many pairs of words can be illustrated as follows:

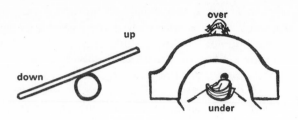

6. Lotto. Here the caller has a complete set of words whilst each child has a card on which appear only some of the words. The caller reads the word and the child with that word on his card responds and is given the word card. It is best if a number of such games are devised on the basis of their difficulty rather than one game with an extremely large number of words. Even the most difficult stage should contain no more than 40 different words.

7. Racing games, treasure hunts and the like can be employed, the child moving one space forward each time he reads a word from a central pile correctly.

Phonic work—traditional approaches

Should the reading scheme in use be of a phonic nature or a mixed methods approach with an ordered introduction of words according to their phonic complexity, there are obvious advantages to be gained from the correlation of all phonic activities to the stage reached by the child in the reading scheme. There is however a danger in this more incidental approach for some steps may be omitted or again sufficient practice may not be given to fit the needs of the individual child. Other teachers prefer to adopt a scheme of phonic work which can be related to the reading scheme and the skills learned employed within it, yet which proceeds independently through the medium of a phonic reader, work books or apparatus and instruction.

Phonic work exists in the bringing together of visual and auditory skills in order to recognize a word. The following steps would seem necessary as a basis for phonic instruction of the traditional type.

1. Be certain that the child has sufficient maturity in auditory discrimination to benefit from the activity.

2. Begin with oral activities making use of rhyming words and alliteration. The game of 'I Spy' and the singing of nursery rhymes and jingles and the rhymes from G. Baldwin's book listed at the end of the chapter can be most helpful here.

3. Link the sound and the visual symbol by the following stages:
   a. Recognition of the sound of the consonant at the beginning of a known word which is phonically regular.
   b. Recognition of the same sound at the end of words.
   c. Recognition of single vowel sounds.
4. As soon as some facility is gained in the above activities the child should be instructed in a technique of blending the sounds into simple words.
5. The teaching of more complex phonic constructions.
6. Never over instruct in phonics and ensure that instruction and activities are enjoyable and immediately usable in reading work.

It is most important that the teacher should ascertain that the early visual and auditory training given has resulted in the appropriate level of maturity for the child to take advantage of phonic instruction. This is important for some children are not ready for phonic work until a good deal of experience has been gained in the use of whole words. Examples of simple tests which can be given in a few minutes to assess the extent of readiness for phonic instruction appear in chapter 14. Children will vary not only in the time at which phonic instruction can be commenced but also in the amount of time which can be usefully given to this activity. Some children will require very little help to advance to the stage of using the aid effectively. Other children will proceed very slowly and some children may not be able to use phonic techniques until they have gained an extensive sight vocabulary.

It will be seen therefore that the teacher must observe the individual child's needs and abilities and make any phonic scheme fit the child rather than the child fit into the scheme. This is stressed for there appears below a chart outlining a scheme of phonic work which is graded according to the level reached in reading age. This is a guide only, for reading age is but one of the many considerations to be taken into account when planning the work of the individual child. It will be seen that the list of sounds suggested contains only the more commonly occurring sounds and is quite small. This has been done for two reasons—firstly when children gain proficiency in phonic techniques they quickly recognize the sound value of the untaught letter combinations and secondly to ask the child to memorize the tremendous number of rules needed to accommodate the vast number of sound/symbol relationships in English would verge on the ridiculous.

Suggested stages for phonic instruction

Reading age	Phonic work
Before 5 years 6 months	Letter identification both visually and aurally as the initial letter of known words and with the help of illustrations. Only the most common sounds of single letters to be used. At this stage it would seem preferable to use letter sounds only and leave the learning of letter names to a later date.
From 5 years 7 months to 6 years 6 months	Identification of letters in any part of the word. Using initial letter and context as a means of word recognition. Analysis and blending of three letter simple words. Words ending in 'ed', 'ing' and plurals in 's'.
From 6 years 7 months to 7 years	Common consonantal digraphs 'ch', 'sh', 'st', 'th', 'wh'. Words ending in 'er' and 'ly'. Practice in blending sounds orally.
From 7 years 1 month to 7 years 6 months	Common vowel combinations 'ee' and 'oo'. (Both sounds as in 'book' and 'shoot'. In some areas the long sound is used in both words). 'ea' as in leaf. The long vowel sounds including 'y' and the rule of the final silent 'e'.
From 7 years 7 months to 8 years	Vowel combinations 'ai', 'ay', 'ie', 'oa'. Vowels plus 'r' as in corn and yard. Consonants followed by 'r' as in drag. Consonants followed by 'l' as in flash. Making long words from short words.

Reading age	Phonic work
From 8 years 1 month to 9 years	Three consonants together as in splash, scratch and threat. Diphthongs 'au', 'aw', 'ou', 'ow' and 'oi'. Division of words into syllables.
Over 9 years	Revision, exercises and occasional testing of proficiency in all above sounds and techniques. Point out the less common rules and the variant sounds of letter combinations as necessary.

Activities for teaching phonics

There are a number of published schemes which can be helpful to the teacher of phonics but most of these have been designed for older children who have experienced difficulty in learning to read. Two schemes worthy of special mention here are Stott's *Programmed Reading Kit* and Tansley's *Sound Sense Books*. Many reading schemes for infant school children have some phonic work included but very often this is not very extensive. Galt and Philip and Tacey both supply helpful apparatus but again it is difficult to compile a complete scheme entirely from such aids. For the infant teacher who wishes to work from books the *Royal Road* scheme of Daniels and Diack or Gattegno's *Words in Colour* could be employed, whereas for the teacher who prefers a published scheme of apparatus, Muriel Reis' scheme *Fun in Phonics* is available. The difficulty which arises from teaching phonics through the use of books and apparatus is that the hearing of the sounds and skill in blending them may be neglected and as a result the most valuable part of phonic instruction could be lost. In using any of the above mentioned items the teacher must ensure that sufficient oral work is done and the skills are in fact learned. Where large numbers in the infant class make it difficult to provide sufficient oral work at the time it is needed by the children, a tape recorder could be employed. A number of published tape schemes are briefly described in chapter 5 and tapes are now available to introduce and accompany the *Sound Sense Books* mentioned above.

Many teachers will no doubt prefer the greater flexibility of a scheme which they have themselves built up and some suggestions for activities and apparatus from which such a scheme could be devised are listed below.

1. Preliminary activities in visual and auditory discrimination such as are mentioned in Chapter 9.
2. Letter recognition and letter sounds.

Most American books on the teaching of reading suggest that capital and lower-case letters and letter names and letter sounds should all be taught from the very beginning. It would seem helpful if the lower-case letters and their most common sound value are taught first as this should reduce the chances of children becoming confused. The letter names are in fact of little value to the reading process and capital letters though less easily confused than lower-case letters are less frequently used in print and if a child writes whole words in capitals in the early stages the occasional placing of a capital letter in the middle of a word seems to persist over a long period.

Suggested activities
1. The matching, sorting, posting and writing of letters.
2. a. Teaching symbol and sound as the initial letter in a simple word. Oral practice with the teacher may be followed by workbook activities. In the example overleaf there is discussion of the picture and the name of the object. The children say this name and listen to the teacher say it. The teacher repeats the word, slowly emphasizing the first letter. The child colours in the large letter and goes over the word with a crayon. The words in Column 1 can be read and discussed and then used for visual and oral recognition of the sound under consideration. Space 2 may be used for writing some of the words from the given list using a colour for the sound being taught. Alternatively this space could be used for practice in the writing of the letter. In space 3 the child is invited to ring those words which contain the sound being considered. The little story in space 4 is read to the children emphasizing the letter and the child may draw an illustration relative to this story in space 5. This work can be accompanied by letter dictation and the game of 'I Spy' and continued in the building of a picture dictionary. The sounds do not necessarily have to be arranged in alphabetical order. Some teachers prefer to teach the vowels first and then as each consonant is added words can immediately be built from them.

	C	cat
	1 cat cap cot cup cab can cut cub cog ccd	**2**
3 bag can cat cap c on dog cod cup		
5	**4** Nicola has lost her cat. It is a black cat with a blue collar on its neck. Nicola is crying, but Mother comes running up the path and calls to Nicola that she has seen the cat climbing a tree.	

	d	dog
	1 dog doll duck dad red did dig and den bed	**2**
3 red doll dog den d bed bag apt dad		
5	**4** Judy has a doll. Judy has dressed the doll in a red dress. Mother gave her the doll today for being a good girl. Judy has asked Mother if she can put her doll to bed.	

e.g. 'a' 'e' 'i' 'o' 'u' 'p 't'.
   pat pet pit pot put it at
   tap tip top pup pop pip

b. Cards can be prepared where the child is given a series of pictures and words from which one letter is missing—he must select the letter and place it in the space. This activity can also be presented in workbook form as in the following example.

Draw a picture of a van	*child writes the word in large letters in this space*
	v ...... n ...... a n v a ......
	The [ ] is by the bus.

c. Simple lists can be compiled where the child has to identify all words which contain the given letter.
b—bag big dog boat blue
r—rat run car net ride
This exercise can also be undertaken orally.

d. Each child is given a list of words, e.g.
bag hit fin ten hop
pet red cut dog fill
Oral questions can be presented such as:
Which word begins with 'p'?
Which words have an 'o' in the middle?
Which word ends in 'l'?

3. The teaching of a system of analysis and blending of sounds can only be done orally but a wide range of written exercises and games can be devised for the practice and consolidation of this activity. The exercises shown above and those on the following two pages are taken from an unpublished series of workbooks (Moyle and

Wrench 1964). These books were carefully programmed to ensure that the introduction of new words was controlled. All the sounds had been introduced previously.

Tom and Len go to camp

New words

Sight words	go	comes	fishing	us
Sound words	t : e : n : t		tent	
	r : o : d		rod	
	l : e : t		let	

Tom and Len go to camp. Tom has a tent and Len has a fishing rod.
Tom puts the tent by the well so they can get water.
A log is by the well so they sit on it. Don comes to the camp.
He runs to Len and Tom. 'Let us go fishing', he says.
Len will go fishing with Don but Tom will not. Tom sits by the tent.
Don gets a fish and Len gets a fish. Don has a big fish but Len's fish is not so big. They get wet as they are fishing.
They come to the camp and sit on the log.
As they sit on the log they get dry in the sun.

These words are missed out of the sentences below.

comes rod fishing camp tent wet well

1. Tom and Len go to *camp.*
2. Len has a............rod.
3. Tom puts the............by the.................
4. Tom has not got a fishing.................
5. They get............as they are.................
6. Don............to the camp.

Find the word which is the same as the first one.

tent	ten	ton	tent	tall
rod	red	rod	run	door
let	led	tell	lot	let

Fill in the missing letters and say the word.

let	rod	tent
et	od	ent
bet	god	b
g	h	d
j	n	l
m	p	r
n	r	s
p		w
s		
w		

Find the stranger

1. red : rod : rid : rip ....
2. let : not : get : wet ....
3. tent : went : want : sent ....

4. As the number of known sounds grows the following activities may be used to vary the manner of presentation.

a. The child may be given a list of words and asked to make new words to rhyme with them. With young children it is useful to give them a clue.

e.g. sat   f............

b. Card games can be devised by printing words with the same endings on cards and making up sets containing a number of groups say 2 or 4 words having the same ending in each group.

c. Wordbits—Here the child is given a number of letters and/or digraphs on small pieces of card from which he can make words.

d. Word slides can be made which are formed from a group of words which have a common sound. (See opposite).

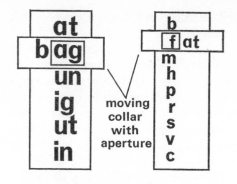

e. Finding little words in big words
e.g. visit – is it   sit
    into – – –   – –
    kitten – – – –   – –   – – –
f. Making compound words

in to—into	car pet—carpet
up on—upon	some thing—something
kit ten—kitten	wheel house—wheelhouse
sand man—sandman	break fast—breakfast

g. Making plurals, comparatives and superlatives in relation to given words.
h. Simple crosswords.
i. Working with a dictionary.
5. At a more advanced stage the division of words into syllables and the combination of lists of syllables into known words is helpful. Three major rules can be given to the children.
    a. All syllables have a vowel sound.
    b. When two consonants occur together the syllable division falls between them.
    c. When only one consonant falls between two vowels the division comes before the consonant.
    At all times the sound of the whole word and its meaning will be emphasized to guard against the possibility of the child reading letter by letter and thus hindering future fluency.

Another approach to phonic teaching
Some teachers may feel the following approach produces the same result as the one described above but without quite so many devised activities. Also it will make it easier to ensure that sounds are not

taught before they are needed and that time is not spent on work which the child has already mastered.

1. The teacher must have a detailed list of the spelling patterns of English and keep a record of those which the child has mastered.

2. The teacher will select and draw attention to particular words as they occur in readers or better still in the child's own written work. This ensures that the word is first met in a meaningful context.

3. The emphasis is on the sounds of units of language, words or syllables, and the letter sound is seen as contributing to that unit. Thus the question becomes not 'What sound does the letter "a" make?' but rather 'What sound does the letter "a" represent in the word "cat" or "play"?'

4. The child builds up a knowledge of key sound units such as syllables and words, rather than rules such as 'the magic "e" makes the vowel before it say its name not its sound.'

The teaching procedure for learning new words may be as follows:

a. Teacher presents the word 'cannot' orally.

b. The child is given two cards with 'can' on one and 'not' on the other.

c. Teacher and child say the two units 'can' and 'not' separately.

d. Teacher says 'cannot' slowly and the child moves the cards together to form the whole word.

e. The child can now be asked to perform the whole operation on his own.

The difficulty some young children have with traditional phonic instruction is that they cannot hold the correct sequence of letter sounds in mind as well as the total word. The suggestions given above ask the child to deal only with synthesis in the first instance and leave the operation of analysis and synthesis together until later.

The child should be encouraged to look for known units as:

'un' - 'less': 'unless'

'v' - 'is' - 'it': or 'vi' - 'sit': 'visit'

It will make it easier for both teacher and child if a dictionary is built using key units for headings. As a new spelling pattern is discovered a new section can be opened and words collected under that heading.

The use of context

The use of context as an aid to word recognition implies that the child is already making an intelligent approach to reading. Contextual clues only come when the child is aware of the meaning of the words and has some knowledge of sentence structure. A limit is therefore placed upon the use of contextual clues by the extent of maturity and development of the child's intelligence. Nevertheless a certain amount of help can be given to the child at the more mechanical level which will remain useful when his knowledge of word meanings and ability to comprehend have increased. Most young children when meeting an unknown word simply stop, whereas their ability to make an intelligent response to this unknown word would be greatly increased if they were to read the remainder of the sentence. The child should be directed to this approach when reading and it can also be fostered by the use of sentences with missing words. The provision of the first letter of a missing word will help young children to combine a use of phonic and contextual clues.

Word study

In the case of the young child most of the work in word study will be the direct outcome of the experiences received and the language work drawn from them. Throughout this language work however every effort will have to be made to help the child realize that so many of our words have more than one meaning and also to clarify the concepts behind the many words which do not refer to objects. Many young children find difficulty with 'front' and 'back' 'up' and 'down' 'here' and 'there' 'over' and 'under'.

Practice can be given in finding words with identical and opposite meanings, in getting the children to give sentences using the words selected. Again lists can be compiled of clothing, food, drink etc, and put under a heading of where they would be kept. Association lists can be made, e.g.

pig – sty – squeal – grunt
lorry – engine – driver – trailer – load – tip
sea – sand – shells – tide – cliffs – boats – fish

Such lists may arise naturally from some centre of interest work and could then be revised by question cards, e.g.

car, coat, peas, hat, bicycle, aeroplane, cake, horse, carrots, tricycle, orange, shoe, apple, cat, fish, bird.
Which can run?............................
Which can fly?........................
Which would you eat?........................
Which do you pedal?........................

Comprehension skills

Most emphasis is usually placed on the ability to report the facts and show an understanding of a passage after the passage has been read. Comprehension and indeed good study habits can be greatly helped if some preliminary work is done before the passage is read. In other words the child reads the passage with a knowledge of its content and his purpose in reading it. This introduction may take many forms according to the type of passage and the age of the children.

1. Some study of words which the children might find difficult.
2. A list of questions might be posed which the child can bear in mind as he reads.
3. Discussion of the illustrations.
4. The reading of the first few sentences followed by a discussion on how the story might proceed.
5. Assistance with the interpretation of any imagery used by the author.

After the reading of the passage or story various types of questions may be posed, e.g.

1. Missing words where the child has simply to find the correct response.
2. Direct questions about the facts given.
3. Questions concerning the opinions and purpose of the author.
4. The child is asked to re-express some sentence or paragraph in his own words.
5. A series of sentences are supplied and the child selects the one which best fits the meaning of a certain given section of the story.
6. Opportunities for the child to express his own views concerning actions or statements within the passage.

General activities to aid word recognition

1. *Flash cards*

Flash cards are widely used to gain proficiency and speed in word recognition among young children. If used for group work it is not a good plan simply to hold up the word and to make the children supply the answer orally. When this is done the quicker and more proficient children overshadow those slower children who are perhaps more in need of the activity. It is more helpful if the children have copies of all the words to be used on their desks and respond to the word held up by the teacher by holding up their own card, and when the teacher is satisfied that each individual child is making the correct visual response the children can say the word together.

The cards can also be used as the basis of games such as lotto where the children have only a selection of the words to be flashed before them and have to respond when a word on their own card is shown. Further use can be made of the cards by adapting ludo and snakes and ladders for use with word cards.

Speed of recognition of known words can be increased by the use of a homemade tachistoscope which can be simply constructed from a cardboard box. An aperture is made at one end through which one child looks whilst another child places the word to be flashed in a small slide at the opposite end. The word will only be seen when the box is illuminated and therefore the time of exposure can be controlled. The children can test each other's proficiency using this aid and the movement of the card, which is distracting when the card is shown by hand, is eliminated.

Sets of flash cards based on words from a reader or from a basic word list can be formed and given to individual children who are asked to arrange them in a sentence or story. This is then copied out by the child and illustrated so that the teacher can quickly check the child's ability to recognize and use the words intelligently.

2. *Word and picture matching*
Wherever possible this activity will be self corrective or errors can be reinforced by frequent inaccurate responses. This can be achieved by making the word and picture fit together in jig-saw style and Philip and Tacey and Waddingtons both have a range of material of this type. Children find great enjoyment from matching work when the pictures and words to be matched are placed on a large board each having its own electrical contact. Touching the correct contacts with the two wires supplied will result in the ringing of a bell or the lighting of a bulb. The children prefer the bell, but the light is more conducive to peace in the classroom.

3. *Language Master*
The blank cards which can be obtained for use with this machine can be designed with illustration and word visually presented while the word itself is recorded upon the tape. The child can pass a card through the machine and listen to the recorded voice of the teacher speaking the word or words several times. He can then check his own learning by recording his own response on the same card. The teacher is able to check the child's work by passing the cards used through the machine. This would seem to be a very useful way of presenting new words which are to be met in the next reader. The

reader is recommended to look also at allied activities suggested in chapters 3, 9, 10 and 11.

Further reading

BALDWIN, G. (1967) *Patterns of Sound* Chartwell Press ·
DURRELL, D. D. (1956) *Improving Reading Instruction* Harcourt Brace and World
MOXON, C. A. V. (1962) *A Remedial Reading Method* Methuen
RUSSELL and KARP (1951) *Reading Aids Through the Grades* Columbia University Press
WEBSTER, J. (1965) *Practical Reading* Evans

CHAPTER 13

Ensuring growth

Reading instruction should not come to an end when the basic mechanical skills have been mastered and the necessity for the reader to have a carefully controlled vocabulary have been left behind. If reading proficiency is to be raised to its highest level in our children then they will need a programme of instruction based on the following specific purposes.

1. The development of comprehension aimed at promoting thoughtful, reflective reading.
2. The ability to vary reading technique according to the type of material being read and the purpose for which the reading was undertaken.
3. The improvement of reading speed and the ability to vary the speed according to the needs of the situation.
4. The ability to interpret specialist subject material, e.g. maps and diagrams.

Developing the ability to comprehend
Some improvement of all related skills in the reading process will be gained simply by reading. Yet growth of skill in comprehension of the written word can be helped by specific practice, by activities involving comprehension from the spoken word, and by work directed towards enlarging vocabulary and the development of concepts. A graded scheme of work will be helpful for, as the ability to comprehend increases, so the child is enabled to move on to more involved work. Working with difficult material also enables the child to increase his ability to comprehend.

Some American texts divide the activity which we generally term comprehension into 40 or 50 types and processes. In most British books of comprehension exercises, particularly those written for primary school children, nothing more than a literal interpretation is called for. Clearly such a low level of interpretation of the printed word is less than sufficient for the child who is constantly asked to use his reading skill to further his own general education through the use of books in projects and discovery approaches. Reading intelligently can also play some part in preparing a child for the continual decision making he will be asked to undertake in adult life. At the present time we give our business men crash courses in order 'to raise their ability to read efficiently but these would be unnecessary if from the early days of reading teaching we built in to our programmes effective approaches to comprehension. In constructing such work the teacher might bear in mind the following aspects of the activity we call comprehension.

1. Literal stage—reporting what the author says in the sequence he presents it. Acting upon simple instructions.

2. Interpretive stage—reexpressing the author's meaning in one's own words, isolating main ideas and supporting ideas, outlining the information or argumentation involved.

3. Evaluative stage—assessing the quality, value, accuracy and truthfulness of what is said by reading between the lines as well as within them and comparing the new material with knowledge accumulated from past experience. This can be undertaken at two levels—the intellectual and emotional.

4. Memorization of those parts thought to add to past reading and experience.

5. Action—using the knowledge gained to answer the questions which provoked the reading in the first place; directing thinking into new areas or new activities; seeking further knowledge or understanding in related areas.

Word study

The child should be encouraged to list any new words he meets in his reading and gain a full understanding of them by the use of a dictionary and discussion with the teacher.

The teacher should analyse lessons and text books used for words which may not be known or involve concepts which have not been fully mastered by the children. Group or class work can then be undertaken where the meanings of these words are discussed and their pronunciation given. These words can then be presented in preliminary exercises where meanings and synonyms have to be selected from a list of alternatives.

In individual work a glossary of the more exceptional words can be pasted into the front of the book. This will enable the child to find the meanings of unknown words much more speedily and simply than if he has to turn it up in the dictionary.

In their silent reading books children often ignore the difficult or unusual word and so build a stumbling block to their own progress. The use of a glossary together with suitable direction and testing of individual reading should overcome this tendency. The testing of silent reading work could include a word definitions test where the child is given a word and asked to select the most suitable definition from a list of alternatives.

Word study will also include some attention to phonic work and word derivation. The application of word analysis techniques to multisyllabic words and the discussion of variant sounds of letter combinations will have a place. The use of prefixes and suffixes, the listing of synonyms, antonyms and homonyms together with the study of words which have multiple meanings all help to increase efficiency in reading. All these activities give help to the child's spelling ability and in turn spelling efficiency is an aid to fluent reading.

Reading for different purposes
1. *Finding information*
In the early stages of work with reference books it is important to provide the child with detailed questions which will direct his search and pre-limit the extent of the material he will collect. The child sent to the bookshelves to find out about 'The ships used by the Saxons' has less chance of collecting his information in an orderly manner or in fact of remembering the details as the child who goes to the same bookshelf with the list of questions such as the following to direct him.

What materials were the ships constructed from?
How big were the ships?
How many people could they carry?
How were the ships propelled?
Why did they place the shields along the sides?
Examine pictures of the ships, then give your own ideas of the character of the Saxon people.

If reference books are to be used adequately the child will need to know how encyclopedias and dictionaries are constructed, how to use the table of contents and the index in order to locate specific information quickly. He will also need guidance on scanning through a page with particular words or phrases in mind which will give him a clue as to where in the book he needs to commence detailed reading.

2. *Reading for study purposes*

Detailed study of texts should be a guided activity, for if the child approaches the reading of the book with some idea of the important facts to be learned he will be able to study more effectively and commit the salient information to memory more easily. Early work in this sphere might take the form of a series of questions to which a number of alternative answers are supplied and the child reads through these, reads the book, then returns and selects the correct answer to each question. At a later stage the child can be supplied with lists of general headings which again are studied before reading the text and elaborated when the reading is completed. This method would seem more fruitful than simply asking for a summary of the book and will lead naturally into a more effective precis technique later in life.

3. *Skimming*

Skimming is a most useful skill for locating specific information, for classification of material and for revision purposes. Skimming can be undertaken simply to see what a text is about, to locate facts or comments on a particular subject or to obtain the main ideas expressed in the text.

The first step is to consider the title and the chapter headings for this will give the reader an indication as to whether the book is likely to be helpful at all to his current purpose. A further indication of the helpfulness of the book may be gained from glancing at any pictures, diagrams or maps which may be included. The next stage is to use the skill of recognizing certain words as suggesting continuation or change in the thought expressed, e.g. 'and', 'also' and 'further' indicate the continuation of the same thought; whereas 'but', 'however' and 'despite', are commonly used to introduce a conflicting argument. Such words will tell the reader whether to read the ensuing passage or to omit it as unnecessary to his purpose.

The next step is to be able to gain the main thought from each paragraph. Here the reader may well gain sufficient information from a reading of the first and last sentences of the paragraph.

Children can be helped towards efficiency in skimming by the following activities.

1. Locating proper names or dates in a passage.
2. Answering questions where the question contains a phrase from the passage.
3. Speed tests in answering questions from a passage, the children competing against their own previous performances rather than against each other.

4. *Plans for study reading*

As children reach a level of fluency their ability to use books effectively for study in depth may be helped by following or adapting one of the plans set out below.

1. *SQ3R* (Robinson 1960)
    i Survey—glance through the material simply to appreciate its structure.
    ii Question what you need to know from the book.
    iii Read thoroughly.
    iv Recall—stop from time to time and see if the content has been memorized. Make brief notes.
    v Revise with the help of notes. Skim through to ensure that nothing important was missed and no wrong impressions gained.

2. *Phased Reading Method* (De Leeuw 1965)
    i Study table of contents.
    ii Decide how much needs to be read and the best order in which to read it.
    iii If reading the whole book glance through the first and last chapters.
    iv Decide what you expect to find which is of use to you.
    v Glance through the remaining chapters.
    vi Read the whole book, making brief notes or marking passages.
    vii After reading each chapter make a brief synopsis.
    viii Make a mental summary of the whole book and check through your notes.

Before using such plans, exercises in trying to express the main idea of a paragraph in as few words as possible are most helpful. This can be followed by making charts of paragraphs under such headings as

1. main idea
2. supporting ideas
3. examples
4. conflicting evidence or argument
5. gaps in information given

6. evidence of suppressed information

7. a statement of author's intent as inferred by the reader.

Increasing speed of reading

To have the ability to read at great speed has value, but nothing of worth is gained unless the child is able to comprehend at this speed. One hears reports of people who profess to be able to read in excess of 4,000 words per minute but this tremendous rate is based on a skimming technique to obtain the gist of a passage rather than a full reading of the passage and is probably obtained by reading vertically rather than from left to right. At an advanced stage such a technique where the eye is fixed upon the centre of the line and thus takes in the word or two on either side of this point can be an advantage but it is unsuitable for children. The reader moves the eye from line to line from the top to the bottom of the page ignoring the words at either end of each line. The more important skill for the child is the ability to read a whole passage quickly yet not at so great a rate that he cannot appreciate the full content of the passage. Speed reading is of course related to the difficulty of the passage and the type of material it contains as well as the ability of the reader. Most people read a novel far more speedily than a textbook. Again all reading teaching will to some extent improve the speed at which the child is able to read. Some specific work can be undertaken which is helpful to promoting improvement in reading rate from a very early stage and which at the same time contributes to a general growth in reading. I would feel however that the use of instruments such as pacers or rate controllers are not suitable for use with children.

1. There should be regular reading of material which is rather below the child's present reading standard, as this allows for growth of a wider span of perception which increases speed. Such work is also helpful as a boost to the child's confidence and in gaining growth in the ability to comprehend the written word.

2. Select readers where the line ending regularly coincides with a sentence or phrase ending to encourage phrase reading.

3. Never allow children to point to individual words as they read but rather encourage them to slide the finger underneath the line at a constant speed.

4. Break the habit of lip movements in silent reading as early as possible.

5. As the children become older their attention can be drawn to

their speed of reading, and they can then be given timed exercises which they can pursue in order to improve this speed. All such exercises should be followed by questions which ensure that the child is not reading so quickly that ability to comprehend the passage suffers. If however it seems that comprehension is suffering from rapid reading it is better to give the child help to improve his comprehension at that speed rather than reduce the speed itself.

Developing a critical approach to reading

In these days of mass media and high pressure advertising it is more important than ever that any literature read should be subjected to all the reader's mental powers. The effectiveness of advertising and propaganda are well known but still many intelligent people accept as truth that which is merely the impression of one observer or the opinion of one commentator. It has become evident that our children need direct instruction if they are to approach reading in a critical manner, for the mere fact of an article having got into print seems to impress upon them that the writer has some magical insight or infallible gifts. The young child comes to reading with an inquiring mind and we must capitalize upon this factor by helping him not only to recognize words and extract knowledge from a passage but also to look for the writer's purpose, to note the things he doesn't say as well as those that are said and finally evaluate the whole by intellectual or emotional judgements in the light of their own total experience. Judgements of this nature demand the exercise of highly intellectual gifts, but they can be encouraged to some extent even among slow learning children.

The first step is to keep alive the inquiring attitudes of the young child by providing books with ever widening horizons. Young children are capable of identifying relationships, of estimating whether a story could be true or whether it is a fairy tale and they should be encouraged to do this. At a more advanced stage two eye-witness accounts of the same incident can be compared and contrasted. Attention can be drawn to differences in the accounts and areas where personal feelings or opinions have distorted what purports to be a factual statement. A passage can be studied in relation to the facts not given by the author. This activity can be undertaken at a very early stage of reading growth by asking the child to list the things he would like to know concerning a certain topic, but which the author of the passage has omitted. At a higher level the child can be asked to look behind the literal meaning of an extract, to consider any implied meaning and evidence of biased opinion on the part of the author. The child can be requested to think of illustrations to prove or disprove claims of advertisements or opinions of authors. A statement such as, 'Most road accidents are caused by carelessness', would prove a rewarding exercise in critical analysis. Many words in the language have gained traditional or emotional overtones and lists of these words could be formed and discussed, for so often propaganda makes very full use of these overtones. Children will quickly respond to the different reactions occasioned by the words 'fat' 'plump' and 'well-built' or 'slim', 'thin' and 'skinny'. Children should also be encouraged to find exceptions to the point of view expressed by an author and to weigh the evidence of the author in the light of these exceptions.

Often children are deterred from critical and elaborative thought during their reading, by many of the comprehension exercises which they are asked to complete, for these exercises ask only for the meaning and summary of the given passage. When selecting books for work in comprehension it will be necessary to look for those which emphasize interpretation and evaluation, if growth in critical reading is to be encouraged.

Reading subject texts
As the child matures he will leave behind the security of the reading scheme with its inbuilt system of gradual growth, controlled vocabulary and repetition. He will be called upon to read subject texts with specialized approaches and technical vocabulary, which may not be explained and will not be repeated with the frequency of new words appearing in a book from the reading scheme. In general specialized texts should underestimate rather than overestimate the reading ability of the child, so that full attention can be given to the layout, the vocabulary and the greater number of facts which need to be noted per page in comparison with a normal reader. The use of a glossary as suggested earlier can be helpful here together with instructions on how to interpret the particular types of diagrams, tables, or maps in the text. At the secondary stage the subject teacher should always be aware of the reading proficiency of her children and help them with the special approaches necessary to reading work in his subject. Mathematics requires very detailed reading; full attention must be given to every word and each step must be built on a complete understanding of previous related steps. The symbols used must all be read and interpreted accurately for all

items have an absolute meaning. In books concerned with social studies, technical vocabulary and diagrammatic representations must be understood but here emphasis must be placed upon a critical approach to sift fact from fiction and assess the worth of arguments of a controversial nature. Perhaps the most important factor in reading a scientific text is the understanding of problem solving techniques, whilst every care must also be given to ensure that the child understands such basic concepts as 'density', 'gravity', 'condensation' and the like.

The emphasis upon scheming our teaching to the interests and enthusiasms of our children has in recent years brought forth the suggestion that with sufficient stimulation and the provision of challenging and exciting experiences and materials our children will no longer need special instruction and exercises to gain a more efficient and intelligent use of books. Recent research however quoted by Robinson (1966) and Smith (1966) suggests that the development of a critical approach and the increase of speed in reading and comprehension only develop satisfactorily when instruction and practice is given in these fields. The formulation of individual programmes incorporating the techniques and skills briefly set out above would be a forbidding task for any teacher. To design a suitable programme for their growth from the work upon which the children are currently engaged would limit the work and probably dull the enthusiasm of the children for activities which would normally excite them. The best answer at the moment would seem to be brief booster programmes using carefully designed materials to teach the necessary skills and then the teacher will ensure that these skills are in fact transferred to all other reading work. The gain produced by 'booster' programmes can easily be lost unless the child is consciously aware of the need for the techniques and can practise them in real situations. If the need for the technique or development of a skill arises from ongoing work in other areas of the curriculum, motivation to complete the task will be increased and the difficulties of transfer decreased. It is recommended that work with the materials described below continues alongside those described in chapter 11.

Reading Laboratories (Science Research Associates)
The first and still the most extensive range of reading laboratories has been produced in America by Dr D. H. Parker. The first laboratory appeared in 1957 and was introduced into Britain in the

early 1960s. One limitation of the laboratories is that they are American and therefore difficulties of spelling arise and the type of literature selected is not always of interest to British children.

A number of experimental trials of these laboratories have taken place in this country to examine their usefulness and test whether the material which was produced in the USA could be equally effective here. There are ten laboratories in all which cover the whole range of reading ability up to the level of the adult. Most trials in this country have been conducted upon Laboratory IIA which covers an approximate reading attainment range of $7\frac{1}{2}$ to 13 years. Two such trials examining rather different features of work with the laboratory have been reported by Pont (1966) and Moyle (1966). Research seems to point to the fact that given $1\frac{1}{2}$ hours work within the laboratory per week for the space of one term, the children will gain an average improvement in comprehension of approximately one year. Further there was no evidence of regression during the following term when little work in English was undertaken. It would appear therefore that it is possible to boost attainment by such a short course and then use the rest of the school year for extra work in the content and creative areas of the curriculum where the skills could be used to great effect.

The material within the laboratory falls under three headings, namely, Power Builders, Rate Builders and Listening Skills. The 144 Power Builders are divided into 12 sections which are graded by colour. Within each colour grade the cards are all of approximately the same difficulty and hence a number of children can use any one grade at the same time. Each Power Builder has an illustration followed by a story or article and follow up questions are set under two headings. The first of these 'How well did you read?' is aimed at accurate comprehension of the passage with some appreciation and insight of the author's purpose, together with an evaluation of statements made. The second heading, 'Learn about words', contains a wide variety of excellent word study exercises and phonic work based on the text. The 144 matched Rate Builders consist of a short passage which the child must read and answer questions on in a limited time, and are aimed at the encouragement of speedy and accurate reading for meaning. The Listening Skills are designed for class use and consist of passages which are read to the class, who then answer questions on them. The child marks and corrects his own work and records his own progress in graph form leaving the teacher free to deal with any errors or misunderstandings which might arise.

The author found the Power Builders and Rate Builders to be most effective, whilst the children found them enjoyable. The material provided for Listening Skills seemed uninteresting in comparison and it is suggested that other passages are recorded on tape so that the children can listen at their own standard in an individual or group, rather than class situation. The most important result to come from the author's experimental work was noted in the results of the observations of the teachers who took part. Both teachers stressed the far wider and more sensitive use of words in conversation and written work and a new enthusiasm for and proficiency in the use of books.

Reading Workshop (Ward Lock Educational)
The first British laboratory-type scheme appeared in 1969 under the editorship of D. A. F. Conochie. The workshop has some aspects in common with the SRA laboratories but is by no means a mere copy of them. Listening skills are not included but the Work Cards and Speed Cards are of a similar format and function to the Power and Rate Builders of the SRA laboratories. There are ten of each of these cards to each colour section. The ten card colour sets represent four to six months' growth in comprehension attainment both in depth and speed.

The manner of working suggested by the authors is also somewhat different. Conochie has suggested that once the child has been placed at his correct point to start work in the workshop he should proceed to work through all the cards which follow. In the SRA laboratories it is suggested that a child can move on to the next section when he is consistently making good scores without necessarily completing all cards within the section. The teacher is of course free to vary the use of the material to suit the needs and abilities of the children and will I feel find it necessary to allow the quicker children to omit some cards whilst the dull may need extra work to move from one stage to the next.

Parker's emphasis was on structured growth of reading skills whereas Conochie's is upon the quality and interest of the literature. Both approaches have their strengths and weaknesses. Parker undoubtedly has too many exercises on phonics and the mechanics of word study and Conochie has overemphasized literal interpretation at the expense of evaluative skills. Whether these latter skills will develop from the stimulus provided by the excellent and wide ranging selection of literature remains to be seen from the trials of the material in the future. For the moment however there can be no doubt that children not only improve their reading at a high rate but also enjoy the work and it may be that the quality of the literature in the Reading Workshop is a major factor.

A second Reading Workshop by the same authors was introduced in 1971. This is similar in format to the first, but covers reading levels of $6\frac{1}{2}$ to 10 years whereas the first covers those of 8 to 13 years. This means that there is a wider coverage, and the school fortunate enough to own both kits will have a wealth of material for the very important 8 to 10 years stage where the two overlap.

Further reading

SMITH, N. B. (1963) Speed reading—benefits and dangers
ROBINSON, H. M. (1963) Developing critical reading *both appear in* J. A. Downing *The First International Reading Symposium* Cassell
FRY, E. (1963) *Teaching Faster Reading* CUP
DE LEEUW, E. and M. (1965) *Read Better, Read Faster* Penguin
MERRITT, J. E. in A. L. BROWN (1967) *Reading: Current Research and Practice* Chambers
MOYLE, D. (1966) *Bulletin of the United Kingdom Reading Association* July
MOYLE, D. (1969) *Some suggestions for achieving transfer of skills learned in a laboratory situation* Everyweek Teachers' Bulletin, spring No 9, summer No 7
PARKER, D. H. (1958) *Schooling for Individual Excellence* Nelson
PONT, H. (1966) An investigation into the use of the SRA Reading Laboratory in three Midlothian Schools in *Educational Research* June
ROBINSON, F. P. (1961) *Effective Study* Harper

CHAPTER 14

Assessing readiness and progress

Few teachers have the psychological background or training to equip them for extensive and expert use of and assessment of the results gained from standardized tests. On the other hand reading is such a complex process that all teachers concerned in instruction in this field should be able to administer standardized tests of reading attainment and the simpler forms of diagnostic tests and be able to take appropriate action on the results gained. It will sometimes be the case that the appropriate action is to refer the child for more thorough diagnostic testing by a remedial teacher or educational psychologist. Our present concern however is in the use of tests as a basis for increased understanding of the development of the individual child and as a result the improvement of the quality of our teaching. As such only those tests which can be adequately employed by the class teacher will be discussed below. The following safeguards must be employed when using published tests.

1. Ensure that you are certain of the purpose of the test and aware of the specific skills it examines. A most helpful text here is S. Jackson *The Teacher's Guide to Tests and Testing* (Longmans 1967.)

2. Adhere strictly to the instructions for administration provided in the manual.

3. Examine the details of the standardization procedure and the sample upon which the norms are based to ensure that the test is a satisfactory one and applicable to your children. This will necessitate some knowledge of statistical terminology.

4. Never teach from the test or help the child in any way for this will invalidate the result and make it impossible for you to apply the test again at a later date.

5. Use tests infrequently. It should be sufficient among normal children to test word recognition and comprehension once each year. Diagnostic tests will normally be given early in school life and

later only when some concern is felt about the progress of an individual child.

6. Care must always be taken in interpretation of test results. They should be looked upon as an indication of the level of attainment reached rather than a figure upon which action can be taken independently of all other considerations. A close watch on the child during performance of a test will give some indication as to whether the result obtained is likely to be an accurate assessment of his attainment.

7. When using diagnostic tests the teacher must be careful to distinguish real disability from the inadvertent error or the lack of maturity. The strengths revealed by the child during his working of diagnostic tests are equally as important as his weaknesses and therefore should be recorded.

8. Individual tests should never be administered where the work can be overheard by other children.

Tests of readiness for learning

Gates-MacGinitie *Reading Readiness Test* (NFER)

Harrison and Stroud *Reading Profiles* (NFER)

Metropolitan Readiness Tests (NFER)

Monroe *Reading Aptitude Tests* (NFER)

There are no British Reading Readiness standardized tests and the four tests named above were all developed in the USA. This means that special care must be taken with regard to the interpretation of results obtained from their use.

1. The average age of the children upon whom standardization took place was 6 years whereas our children commence school in the term in which they become 5.

2. Age norms are not usually given but the results are averaged to give an indication of whether the child is ready for formal instruction or not. It would seem important however to look at scores on the individual sub-tests for here the teacher will gain knowledge concerning the development and maturity of the various skills involved in reading.

3. Some questions relating to language development are biased towards American children.

4. They are designed as group tests and therefore great care will be necessary to administer them to children of 5 years of age.

The many difficulties involved lead one to suggest that the use of such extensive material is better reserved for those few children who give the teacher concern during their early days at school and that the teacher design some simple material which can be given quite quickly to small groups or individual children. Some suggestions for such material appear below but it must be remembered that this type of approach is merely a structuring of teacher observation—it will not have the validity of a standardized test but will be helpful in that it can give the teacher an indication of what particular help the child needs to progress towards reading. Some material should also be worked through with those children who have begun to read before commencing school for they may need help in specific areas in order to proceed with reading instruction successfully.

Before proceeding to observe and test children it is helpful to have a system of recording the information gathered. In an earlier chapter the use of a book for each individual child was suggested in preference to a series of cards. If this plan were adopted record forms could be duplicated and placed in the front of such a book so that they are always readily available when working with the child. There is of course little point in recording information concerning children unless it is used as a basis for future action. The following plan might prove helpful to the teacher in designing her own record form.

Check list for reading readiness

Name................................... Address...................................

Date of birth...................................

Date of entry to school...................................

Home environment...................................

....

Date of observations...................................

1. Physical readiness
   Does vision appear normal?...................................
   Is hearing normal?...................................
   Is articulation and pronunciation clear and free from gross errors?...................................
   Is he able to cut out, use tools, control a ball and crayon?...................................
   Is he apparently healthy and free from fatigue?...................................
2. Psychological readiness
   Is the child interested in language?...................................
   Can he express himself clearly?...................................
   Is his vocabulary suited to the reading materials which will be available for him to use?...................................

Does he enjoy stories?...............
Is his play normal for his age?...............
Can he represent an idea by a drawing?...............
Can he memorize a short song or poem?...............
Can he concentrate on a single piece of work for five or more minutes?...............
Can he view items in order from left to right?...............
Can he interpret pictures?...............
Can he predict possible outcomes for a story?...............
Does he realize that printed symbols can be associated with the spoken word?...............
3. Social and emotional readiness
Can he work with other children?...............
Does he listen to others?...............
Can he work on his own?...............
Does he take reasonable care of materials?...............
Does he usually complete a task?...............
Is he well adjusted to other children?...............
Does he cooperate with adults readily?...............

A series of columns can be drawn alongside these headings and a half-termly check made of the child's progress. The headings are designed to prove helpful in suggesting areas of concentration which could hasten the start of reading; it is not necessary to have a 'yes' beside each heading before allowing the child to start reading work. The teacher will also have to add a series of other items which relate to the approach to be employed and the materials available for the child to use. These will no doubt arise in relation to the sections discussed below. For example if language experience work is to play a major part, considerable observation of the child's ability and interest in communicating his thoughts in language to others must take place.

Language development
Note whether the child is able to speak in sentence form and express himself lucidly. Pay particular attention to any speech defect which may be present and if a child has a stammer, the type of situations in which this tendency is most and least obvious. The earlier a child with speech difficulties is referred to the speech therapist the more hope there is of a complete cure of the defect. Many young children however have difficulty in enunciation of 'r', 's' 'c' and 'l' which usually disappears without any special treatment.

The child's vocabulary could be tested by compiling a set of simple pictures which could be used in two ways.

a. Show the child a picture and ask him to name it or say what activity is being carried out.

b. Group the pictures and ask the child to select one from the group which illustrates a given word or sentence.

Common nouns and verbs can be taken from the reading scheme used in the school, McNally and Murray's Key Word List or from Edwards and Gibbons' *Words Your Children Use*, whilst simple pictures for the purpose can be obtained from Philip and Tacey's sets of gummed stamps. It is a good idea to grade the words both for variety and difficulty in order that the type and quality of previous language experience may be ascertained.

A brief list of suggested words appears below.

Nouns	Verbs	Colours
dog	skipping	white
bus	climbing	black
horse	digging	red
train	falling	yellow
lorry	cutting	brown
seaside	burning	grey
caravan	painting	purple
soldier		
banana		
whale		
cowboy		
umbrella		
plough		
square		

Can the child interpret and act upon simple directions such as:
Come to me.
Bring your pencil to me please.
Please get some paper from the cupboard by the door.
Should the child have some weakness in language development use can be made of the tests in the appendices to A. F. Watts' *Language and Mental Development of Children*. These simple, fairly informal tests will give guidance as to the nature of the weakness and suggest the type of help needed by the child.

Picture interpretation

1. Give the child a simple picture and ask him to point out certain objects.

2. Ask the child to describe what is happening in a picture.

3. Give the child 3 or 4 pictures which form a simple story sequence and ask him to place them in the correct order.

Should the child be able to undertake all the tasks under the above two headings it is likely that his language development and general knowledge are sufficient for the child to read a simple book providing that his other skills have matured equally. If however there appear to be a number of gaps then it is wise to give the child further time to widen his experience and develop his use of language.

Visual skills

1. *Coordination of hand and eye*

a. The child can be asked to trace the path of a mouse who is going down a hole to find a piece of cheese. Whilst the child traces the path with a pencil the teacher should note the speed of accomplishment of the task and the ability of the child to progress smoothly and keep his pencil equidistant from the given lines together with any difficulty shown in changing direction.

b. Copying figures. This activity includes visual memory and can be applied with the given figure present or by requesting the child to draw the figure after the specimen has been displayed for a short interval.

c. Copying letters. Should the child be unable to copy letters, or perform very poorly on any of the above tasks he should be given

194

exercises of a similar nature; use mazes, join dots to form pictures and work with templates and tracing paper.

2. Recognition and orientation

The selection of two identical pictures, shapes or letters from a group of similar illustrations. See below.

Any difficulty at any stage in this type of task can usually be overcome by means of matching exercises, copying, tracing and writing.

3. Handedness and eyedness

a. Establish which is the preferred hand and foot, particularly noting if these are not on the same side of the body.

b. Establish whether the child has a dominant or leading eye and whether or not this is on the same side of the body as the preferred hand.

c. Is the child able to use the terms left and right with accuracy.

Not all adults have in fact a clearly established preference in hand and eye and the lack of a dominant eye does not necessarily form a stumbling block to reading progress. Some children are rather late in establishing such a dominance and therefore it is suggested that no action be taken upon the knowledge gained from these observations at this early stage. However should a lack of dominance coincide with a grave weakness in visual perception and orientation the child should be given a wide programme of visual activities and should he not respond to these further medical and psychological observation should be requested.

Eye dominance can be fairly easily observed by giving the child a large cone having a wide aperture at one end and a small one at the other. The child is requested to look through the wide end at the teacher's face and the teacher should be able to see only one of the child's eyes and this will be the dominant one. In some children further testing will be necessary to make a confident statement concerning eye dominance.

Auditory discrimination
1. Ask the child to clap a simple rhythm after a demonstration.
2. Can the child distinguish between a high and a low note?
3. Can the child repeat letter sounds and words?
4. Can the child recognize words which rhyme in a simple verse spoken by the teacher?

Phonic Readiness
In many children skill in the identification and use of sounds develops rather later than their ability to recognize a whole word. To identify the extent of growth of this skill in order to devise a programme which commences at the appropriate point the following tests are suggested.

1. Which of the following words which I am going to say sound the same at the end?
cat   dog   bat
2. Which of these words has a different ending from the others?
moon   spoon   bite
3. Which of these words has a different sound at the beginning?
bag   lid   ball   bin
4. Which of these words begins with 'f'?
doll   first   cat
5. Which of these words has a different sound in the middle?
big   dip   log   pin
6. Can you tell me what word these sounds make?
d – o – g

7. Can you tell me some words which begin with 'b'?
8. Can the child associate the letter symbol with the letter sound?

Should the child be able to make auditory discriminations yet not be able to tackle any of the above, the tests themselves will indicate the type of activity which the child is now ready to undertake.

Tests of reading attainment
Most of the standardized reading tests available provide the teacher with a reading age or a comprehension age. Such scores are of limited value when considered in isolation from other factors. For a full assessment of the attainment of a child these scores must be compared with each other, with fluency and expression noted when the child is reading from a book and with the rate of progress being made. Such tests have a further use however in that they may often give a pointer to particular weaknesses which had not fully come to light in the child's everyday reading work. Any apparent weaknesses noted can then be further examined by the use of diagnostic materials. The uses, advantages and disadvantages of some of the more popular tests will be discussed below.

Most tests call their result a reading age but the nature of the task set by the test often varies considerably. Before using any test or trying to interpret a test result make sure that you are clear as to what the test is really testing. For example, very different skills are being employed in working through a word recognition test and a sentence completion test and any one child may achieve quite different results in two such tests given on the same occasion.
Graded Word Reading Test Burt (ULP) Reading age from 4 to 15 years
Graded Word Reading Test Schonell (Oliver and Boyd) 5 to 15 years
Graded Word Reading Test Vernon (ULP) 5 to 18 years

These three tests were compared and restandardized by Vernon in 1947 and a table giving the comparison of equivalent levels of difficulty of the tests at all stages from 5 to 20 years appears in *Reading Ability*, Pamphlet 18 of the Ministry of Education, HMSO (1950) which is unfortunately out of print, but the effort involved in searching out a copy in the local public library will be well worth the trouble. Apart from bringing the three tests into line it enables the teacher to use the three tests interchangeably and yet still compare with reasonable accuracy the scores made by a child from one testing to the next. Further the restandardization was related to the Ministry surveys of reading ability at the national level and therefore it is possible to make some allowance for the reported growth in reading attainment over the years 1948 to 1964—this cannot of course be a statistically accurate procedure.

These tests are individual tests of a mechanical nature, testing the ability of the child to recognize a word without the aid of any context clues. All three tests are arranged in stages, each stage consisting of ten words. In the original standardization of the tests each group of ten words represented one year of growth in reading attainment. The first 20 words of the Burt test are perhaps best viewed as representing 0·05 of a year each from 5 to 6 years. With this exception the formula for the calculation of the reading age on all the tests is

$$RA = \frac{\text{Number of words read correctly}}{10} \text{ plus } 5 \cdot 0 \text{ years}$$

It is suggested that the test results are recorded in full and not discarded when a note has been made of the resultant reading age achieved. If this is done then the point at which the test can be commenced will be shown for the next occasion upon which a child is tested with a consequent saving of time. Also if actual errors are written in decisions can be made with regard to any necessary diagnostic and remedial work. A sheet may be prepared with dots spaced in groups of 10 like the words on the tests for the same form

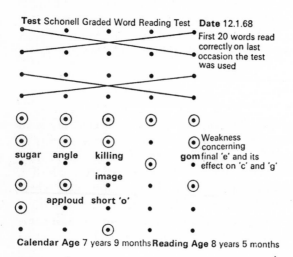

Test Schonell Graded Word Reading Test   Date 12.1.68

First 20 words read correctly on last occasion the test was used

sugar   angle   killing   gom   Weakness concerning final 'e' and its effect on 'c' and 'g'

image

apploud   short 'o'

Calendar Age 7 years 9 months Reading Age 8 years 5 months

can be used for all three tests. Words read correctly could be marked with a circle and errors made could be written in the position of the word on which the incorrect response was made.

A grid for the easy comparison of results over the years can be provided as follows and this also should be placed at the beginning of the child's reading record book.

Date	Test	CA	RA	Standard Score	Teacher's Initials

Together with such a grid there should be the child's date of birth and any assessments of intelligence that have taken place. A separate column is supplied for those tests which yield a standard score rather than a reading age.

Prose and sentence reading tests

Analysis of Reading Ability M. D. Neale (Macmillan) Reading age 6 to 14 years

Some teachers prefer the type of individual test which places the child in a more normal reading setting. The test which best fits this desire is Neale's Analysis of Reading Ability. This test consists of short stories of increasing difficulty each preceded by an illustration. The test allows for the calculation of ages for speed, reading accuracy and comprehension and has three parallel forms. There is a most detailed form for recording responses which is helpful in gaining some diagnostic knowledge. The test takes somewhat longer to administer than a word recognition test but if this time can be spared, the added information gained is worthy of the effort.

Simple Prose Reading Test Schonell (Oliver and Boyd) Reading age 5 to 9 years

This test consists of a single story, the vocabulary of which increases in difficulty as the story proceeds. The reading of the story may be timed and comprehension questions are supplied. The test seems to be fully satisfactory only in the upper half of the age range for which norms are given and the child in the lower half of the range must always end the test with a feeling of frustration as the story becomes too difficult for him to read.

Standard Reading Test 1 Daniels and Diack (Chatto and Windus) Reading age 5 years 2 months to 9 years
This test consists of 36 questions composed of words whose increasing difficulty has been judged mainly on phonic considerations. Questions 1 to 26 receive 3 marks each if read correctly, no marks are credited for the answers to the questions, no marks are given if the child makes any mistakes. In items 27 to 36 one mark is given for an accurate reading and one mark for a correct answer to the question. The age-range of the test is rather limiting and its phonic nature worries many teachers. In practice I have not found that the test does in fact discriminate to any marked degree against those children who have received little phonic training.

Holborn Reading Scale Watts (Harrap) Reading age 6 to 14 years
This test consists of 33 sentences which grow in difficulty. The sentences express a thought very clearly and the reading age gained includes a measure of linguistic development as well as mechanical skill. It usually takes less time to administer than Neale's test but there is no speed rating nor the same opportunity to make observations of a diagnostic nature. A comprehension test for children over the age of 7 years can be administered orally whilst the child selects from the appropriate sentence on the test sheet the required answer. The questions and norms for both sections of the test appear in the test handbook or can be consulted in Watts' *Language and Mental Development of Children*—(Harrap 1944).

All the above tests produce reading ages which are readily comparable. In testing large numbers of children with two or more of the tests at a single interview scores rarely differed by more than 3 to 4 months.

Group tests of reading attainment
Group tests are far more economical in use from the point of view of the teacher's time and the deployment of staff within the school.

They are not however as helpful as the individual test for the following reasons.

1. The attainment range covered by a group test is usually more restricted.

2. The individual child cannot be observed in the detailed manner possible in the individual test situation.

3. They are not usually as helpful in indicating the necessity of diagnostic work.

4. They are less likely to give an accurate assessment of attainment particularly among young children or those who lack the ability to work independently of teacher guidance.

5. Most group tests are graded and in the group situation it is difficult to ensure that the child does not reach the stage of frustration as the material becomes too difficult for him.

Group tests are perhaps most useful as a preliminary survey aimed at the isolation of those children with superior or inferior attainments in order that they may be given further guidance.

Southgate Group Reading Tests V. Southgate (ULP)
Word Selection   Test 1 (3 parallel forms) Reading age 5 years 9 months to 7 years 9 months
Sentence Completion   Test 2 (2 parallel forms) Reading age 7 years to 9 years 7 months
Test 1 examines word recognition skills in the early stages whilst Test 2 involves a measure of comprehension. Both tests are relatively easy to administer and mark. The tests take 20 to 25 minutes each to administer. Test 1 is untimed whereas Test 2 has a time limit of 15 minutes after the 5 practice examples have been worked. The tests were published in 1959 and 1962 respectively and thus the norms provided are more up to date than those for most of the individual tests available.

Group Reading Assessment Spooncer (ULP) Reading age 6 years 3 months to 11 years 7 months
This test published in 1964 has a rather wider age-range than most group tests and the raw score can be converted to a reading age within the range given above or to a standard score for children whose chronological age lies between 7 years 8 months and 9 years.

The test is in three sections. Part One is untimed but including examples takes rather less than 15 minutes. The children are given a word orally and they must underline the word having selected it from a group of five given words on their test sheet. Part Two is timed at 8 minutes and including the working of examples takes some twelve minutes to administer and is composed of sentence completion exercises. Part Three is timed at 5 minutes and takes approximately 8 minutes including the examples. The child is given a word and has to find a word or words from the list which follows which sounds exactly the same although it has a different spelling and meaning. The resultant score therefore is a mixture of attainment in word recognition and comprehension and some indication as to specific difficulties in either of these two fields can be extracted from the test sheets.

Reading Test AD Watts (NFER) Reading age 7 years 6 months to 11 years 1 month
This is a test of the sentence completion type first published in 1958 and more carefully standardized than most other comparable tests. It is therefore most useful for survey purposes particularly with children in the second year of the junior school. The resultant standard score, reading ages are not given, is based upon a mixture of attainment in word recognition and comprehension.

Young Reading Test Young (ULP) Reading age 6 to 11 years
This test first appeared in 1969. It has two parallel forms timed at 15 minutes and consists of tests of word recognition and sentence completion. It is therefore a test of reading accuracy most useful for children of 7 to 10 years of age. The raw score is converted to a quotient rather than a reading age.

Secondary Reading Tests Bate (NFER) 11 to 15 years
There is no really satisfactory test for the average secondary school child published in this country though there are a number of American tests which are helpful if carefully interpreted. The Secondary Reading Tests are in the process of standardization and should prove to be most helpful material when this task is completed. The three tests, namely Vocabulary, Comprehension and Speed take approximately 75 to 80 minutes to administer and therefore would be better administered in three separate sessions. Provisional information with regard to the interpretation of the scores obtained can be forwarded to the teacher if application is made to the Research Officer (Tests) at the National Foundation for Educational Research.

Group tests of comprehension

Silent Reading Tests A and B Schonell (Oliver and Boyd) Reading age
6 years 7 months to 13 years 9 months

These two tests are not strictly parallel forms but they do cover
almost the same range of reading attainment. Form A is timed at
9 minutes and Form B at 15 minutes. Both consist of short paragraphs which the child must read in order to answer the question at
the end. In practice I have found that children seem to gain a slightly
higher score on Form A than on Form B.

G.A.P. Reading Comprehension Test McLeod (Heinemann) Reading
age $7\frac{1}{2}$ to $12\frac{1}{2}$ years

This test originally produced in the USA in 1965 was published
in Britain after a complete anglicization exercise undertaken by
D. Unwin in 1970. The test is based on cloze technique where the
child has to complete a number of spaces in a passage of prose
without the help of a list of words from which to select. The test
takes 15 minutes to administer. Cloze procedure appears to be one
of the most complete tests of all the skills involved in effective
reading. The seven passages in this test appear to be rather too brief
for the technique to be a really searching test of thoughtful reading.

Test 12 Standard Reading Tests Daniels and Diack (Chatto and
Windus) Reading age 6 to 14 years

This test is given the title of a graded test of reading experience but is
in essence a test of comprehension. It contains 50 graded items of the
sentence completion type and is untimed, though 20 to 25 minutes
is usually sufficient to ensure that all the children have completed all
the questions they are capable of doing.

Manchester Reading Comprehension Test Senior 1 Wiseman and
Wrigley (ULP)

This is the only group test of reading standardized in this country
for the higher reaches of attainment in the secondary school. It was
standardized in Manchester on a group of children of 14 to 16 years,
but can be used to advantage with children on both sides of these
age limits.

Further reading

BUROS, O. K. (1968) *Reading Tests and Reviews* Gryphon Press
DANIELS, J. C. and DIACK, H. (1964) *The Standard Reading Tests*
Chatto and Windus

DE HIRSCH, K. (1967) *Predicting Reading Failure* Harper and Row
JACKSON, S. (1967) *The Teachers' Guide to Tests and Testing* Longmans
SCHONELL, F. J. (1942) *Backwardness in Basic Subjects* Oliver and Boyd
TANSLEY, A. E. (1967) *Reading and Remedial Reading* Routledge and
  Kegan Paul
WATTS, A. F. (1944) *The Language and Mental Development of
  Children* Harrap

CHAPTER 15

Reading difficulties

Despite the fact that very few children leave our schools unable to read at all there are still all too many who have gained insufficient proficiency and/or interest in reading for them to consider reading as a useful and enjoyable activity in adult life. The lack of use of books and the reading skill gained inevitably means that their skill in reading will decline over the years. More than this poor reading attainment limits work in other areas of the curriculum and the sense of failure occasioned by poor attainment breeds poor social attitudes.

Once a child's attainment in reading has fallen appreciably below the level normally expected for a child of his age and abilities his chances of catching up are very small. Effort therefore must be concentrated upon prevention, not only to gain a higher standard of reading but also to prevent the sense of failure and the resultant lowering of the emotional attitudes and intellectual aspirations of the child. In order to prevent retardation in reading we need to know something of the causes, to recognize the symptoms early and then provide well planned remedial or compensatory activities in an effort to surmount them.

The causes of backwardness in reading

The causes of backwardness in reading are often complex, indeed Roswell and Natchez (1964) assert that there is never a single cause but always a combination of adverse factors, which are interrelated. Often the original causative factors are difficult to isolate for frequently a symptom exhibited could equally well be the result of failure as it could the cause of the failure. This is particularly true when the child exhibits emotional difficulties. It is necessary in order to design good remedial treatment to have as full a knowledge as possible of the causation of reading difficulty and so emotional difficulties if exhibited by a child must be traced back to their origin. Was the child emotionally immature in the pre-school years? Was any emotional instability noticed during early days at school or did they appear later? Is there any history of emotional instability among his immediate family? Here we see the importance of detailed observation and recording from the beginning of school life being of great help in tracing the origin of any difficulties which the child experiences at a later date.

In the following brief discussion of the aetiology of backwardness in reading, possible causes will receive individual consideration but it must de remembered that causation is usually a result of two or more adverse factors.

Low intelligence

We noted earlier that reading ability and intelligence are positively correlated and quite highly so in the early school years. Schonell (1942) found backwardness in reading more prevalent among dull children than among average and bright children. Malmquist (1958) though noting an average IQ rating of poor readers some 11 points below that of the average for the total sample, felt that intelligence level was of much less importance than social and environmental factors. Again Wall (1945 and 1946) and Houghton and Daniels (1966) have shown quite clearly that children deemed ineducable on the basis of their intelligence quotient could in fact learn to read.

It would seem fair to conclude that a low intelligence level does not prevent a child from reading but it will almost certainly mean that he will start to read later than the average child; he will progress more slowly and need more careful guidance. The child of low ability therefore should not have difficulty if the instruction given is based on his own personal developmental pattern, his progress carefully observed, and his instruction is sympathetically imparted. It is obvious that if a sense of failure is added, by lack of carefully planned work in school, to his meagre innate ability the situation becomes rather difficult to remedy.

Dyslexia

A small number of children appear to have very grave difficulty in perceiving the printed word. This condition may be further complicated by poor speech, lack of an established cerebral dominance or hyperactivity. Such children have often in the past been referred to as being word-blind but most authorities today refer to them as suffering from dyslexia or specific developmental dyslexia. Estimates of the number of such children in the USA have been as high as 10 or 15 per cent of the population. The only survey which has really tried to isolate these children in this country has been the one by Tizard in the Isle of Wight which resulted in a figure of 1·5 per cent whilst Morris (1966) in the Kent Survey felt that no evidence had been uncovered by this survey to suggest that such a condition existed at all. Some authorities consider that this condition is rooted in some disfunction of the brain due to damage at birth or through illness. The medical knowledge and tests necessary to establish or refute this theory are not as yet available to us and therefore much of the work written round this topic is at present suspect. Whilst some maintain that the condition is based in damage to the brain others such as Birch (1962) have suggested that quite a number of these children have not in fact suffered some irreparable damage but rather are the victims of uneven or slow maturation of the neurological mechanisms. Benton (1962) goes even further and brings evidence that many children in this classification have outgrown their difficulties by the age of nine or ten years.

The teacher must not therefore fall into the trap of supposing that any child who seems unable to memorize letter or word shapes is suffering from brain damage and as such will not respond even to the best and most sympathetic teaching. It must be stressed that many children have such difficulties in a milder form often from emotional causes whilst others whose difficulties have been most severe have in fact learned to read at a later stage in their school life. Again some children who have been proved to have brain damage which interfered with the normal functioning of their perceptual processes have eventually learned to read. The emphasis must be placed therefore on careful diagnosis along the lines suggested by Tansley (1967) and an expertly designed programme of compensatory activities.

Physical conditions

All learning takes place more easily when the child is in full health. Illness, poor diet and lack of sleep all have an effect upon the ability of the child to learn to read. In these days most major defects of vision, hearing and motor abilities have received some attention in the pre-school years, but a full correction of the defect may not have been possible. Many minor defects of sight and hearing may have escaped notice and the teacher must always be on the look-out for any children who may be having difficulty from such a cause.

Visual and aural discrimination

Thackray (1971) showed tests of visual and auditory discrimination applied at the commencement of school life to correlate more highly than any other tests with reading attainment at a later date. Most children have in fact gained sufficient mastery of the perceptual processes in order to begin reading by the time they commence school. This fact has led to teachers supposing all children to be equally mature in these skills and also to a reluctance to encourage growth of these skills by specific activities during the early stages of reading instruction. Those children who through lack of cerebral dominance, emotional instability or poor environmental conditions have not achieved the normal level of maturity in visual and aural skills may be unable to appreciate and memorize shapes and the orientation of letters. All children will read somewhat better if attention is given to the development of the perceptual processes, but for those children whose perception is weak specific training in these skills must precede any attempt to give formal reading instruction. On the other hand poor orientation reversals and poor hand/eye coordination can often be caused by reading failure as well as being a cause of it. It will be necessary therefore to have a full knowledge of the child's development in order to detect his true difficulties, and not simply an investigation of perceptual disorders which may only be a symptom and not a cause of failure.

Language difficulties

Weakness in any of the language arts will inevitably lead to difficulty with the reading process but it is obvious that a child who has difficulty with spoken language is at a disadvantage in learning to read from the very beginning. Lack of ability in the use of language can stem from three different sources namely, low innate ability, speech defects and a poor linguistic environment. Crookes and Greene (1963) found a definite association between speech defects and poor reading ability. Speech defects may stem from brain damage, defects of the speech organs, faulty breathing, emotional troubles, poor hearing or weak auditory discrimination. A medical examination followed by psychotherapy or speech therapy may be necessary before reading instruction can be undertaken with success.

Bernstein (1961) has shown how the quality of the child's environment can affect his language development. The child who lacks a satisfactory home background is liable to be deprived of both experience and linguistic growth and whenever this is suspected a compensatory programme should be devised in order to supply the background necessary to good reading progress which the child has been denied. Such children will often be discovered by the comparison of their scores in performance and verbal tests, the latter usually being several points below the former.

Personality and emotional factors
In order to achieve adequate performance in a complex activity such as the reading process it is necessary first to have a high degree of personality integration and emotional stability. It is extremely difficult to assess the extent to which emotional attributes affect reading progress for they rarely can be cited as a sole causative factor. Nevertheless emotional difficulties are a feature of so many children who make poor reading progress that it must be acknowledged as a cause of failure. Robinson (1946) discovered that 60 per cent of a small group of poor readers were suffering from emotional disturbance and felt that in 43 per cent of the cases that emotional factors were a definite cause of failure.

The class teacher by the nature of her training and responsibilities will only be able to help those children whose emotional problems are relatively minor ones, and even this will be a lengthy process. The more serious cases of emotional instability should receive psychiatric treatment.

Many children fail in reading because the instruction given and/or the materials used are inappropriate to their personality traits and interests. Increasingly it is realized that effective teaching depends as much on its relationship to the personality and emotional needs of children as on its appropriateness to their abilities.

Environmental factors
Environmental influences are frequently important in a number of causative factors. The child from the home with a poor educational atmosphere may suffer linguistic deprivation whilst many emotional problems in children are directly traceable to poor parental relationships. The child's home life and the type of area in which he lives may have a direct influence upon preparation for and attitudes towards work in school. There are still many parents who are entirely devoid of any educational aspirations on behalf of their children and some who consider school life a complete waste of time. Again the child whose home is satisfactory can gain unhelpful attitudes from his peers and come to school with his mind unreceptive to the efforts of the teacher.

Where such conditions exist the teacher can only hope for slow and small improvements for the re-education of the adults concerned is basic to a complete reversal of the situation. The teacher must not only know the nature of the environment and endeavour to compensate for such items as lack of experience and parental affection but must also endeavour to gain the confidence and aid of the parents.

There are of course parents whose offences are entirely opposite to those listed above, far from ignoring their children and being uninterested in their children's progress they place their children under considerable emotional strain by demanding progress in excess of the child's ability. Usually such parents can be helped to see the issues involved more clearly and the teacher must ensure that such pressures upon the child are relieved before serious emotional problems result from them.

Factors in the school

Morris (1966) drew attention to a number of factors present within the schools which seemed unhelpful to reading progress especially if the child was already backward. It seemed that poor readers were frequently given the poorest accommodation and materials and the inexperienced or weak teacher. A number of teachers of backward children did not work with such children from choice and many had little training or experience in teaching the early stages of reading. Again few teachers had ever used any diagnostic materials and it was felt that reading instruction was often very poorly organized. Such observations inevitably brought many protests from teachers and in fairness it must be said that there has been some improvement since the time of the Kent Survey in both provision and quality of instruction.

If the numbers of children who experience reading failure are to be further reduced then the following items will require attention.

1. Classes within the infant school must be reduced in size.

2. A wider understanding of the nature of individual differences.

3. An improvement of the class teacher's understanding of the psychology of the reading process.

4. A more systematic and scientific approach to reading instruction which is based firmly in a knowledge of the developmental pattern of each individual child.

5. A wider use of diagnostic materials and earlier reference of children whom the teacher considers are likely to fail to the school psychological service.

6. The continuing observation of children who have experienced difficulties in the past.

7. A wider use of modern aids and equipment which the teacher can structure into the reading programme and so extend the amount of individual help which can be given to the children.

The provision of specialist reading teachers within the junior and secondary schools and a healthy attitude of all teachers towards backward children and their problems.

Helping the child who has failed

So complex are the causes of backwardness in reading that it is unlikely that its occurrence will be completely eradicated in the foreseeable future by the simple expedient of improving provision and instruction at the infant school stage. Prevention will of course always be preferable to an attempt to cure at a later stage. Some studies, notably Collins (1961) and Lovell (1963), have suggested that attempts to provide a cure in the form of remedial reading instruction are largely unsuccessful. Kellmer Pringle (1961) produced evidence that remedial instruction could in fact be very successful. The differing evidence with regard to the success of remedial work seems to point to the fact that success is relative to the type of child selected and the quality of the instruction given.

The major criticisms of remedial work in the past would appear to be:

1. A lack of adequate diagnosis which results in the treatment of symptoms rather than real difficulties.

2. The frequent complete isolation of the help given from the normal work of the classroom.

3. Too much skill training and not enough skill-using.

4. Specialist help being withdrawn too early.

5. The lack of a model for planning remedial help.

6. Remedial help frequently begins too late.

Below an attempt is made to provide the principles of a working model for remedial reading work in the normal class situation which the author feels is more appropriate for most children than withdrawing small groups for occasional sessions with a remedial reading teacher.

1. Aims

The aims of remedial reading work should be the same as those for the child making normal progress, for the term remedial suggests

.that the child can be rescued from his difficulties. The aim will be to help the child to become an efficient reader, to use his reading to good effect in work or leisure and to gain satisfaction and enjoyment from the activity. If this aim is accepted the remedial work undertaken will emphasize not only the subskills of reading but also the uses of the reading process.

2. Diagnosis

All too often diagnosis has concentrated upon the search for difficulties and weaknesses. It is equally important to discover the child's strengths and interests. Further diagnosis should not be merely a battery of tests to precede the help given, but should be a continuing process so that the changing needs of the child can be immediately reflected in the work he undertakes. In this context informal observations are just as important as the more scientific' published diagnostic tests.

In order to prevent too much time being spent needlessly in testing and observing children with reading difficulties, a plan must be followed. The correct approach to a given child can often be ascertained quite quickly for only a minority of children—those with severe emotional, perceptual, and linguistic difficulties—who fail in reading have difficulties of a grave nature which need to be examined by a psychologist with specialist diagnostic instruments.

Stage 1
A description of the child's present reading attainment and habits. Reading attainment tests such as those described in chapter 14 can be used for this purpose but such information should be supplemented by observing the child in normal reading and writing situations. Such observations should take note of any imbalance between word recognition and the understanding of what has been read, the child's attitude to the task and powers of concentration upon it.

A survey of reading and writing errors can be made under the following headings:
1. Reversal of letters or words.
2. Mispronunciations.
3. Substitution of one letter by another.
4. Omission of letters.
5. Addition of letters.

Stage 2

This section of the diagnosis will be carried out simultaneously with Stage 1. Having described the nature of the child's reading behaviour it is necessary to place this knowledge in the context of the whole child, paying particular attention to the following types of information.

1. Nature of the child's home environment.
2. His educational history.
3. His oral language development.
4. Any notable differences in attainment, attitudes and concentration between reading and other work in school.
5. Relationship with other children both in and out of the classroom.

At this point it should be possible to make decisions as to what are the possible causes and nature of the child's difficulties. Some will appear to show little evidence of any specific disability or difficulty and may benefit immediately from a coaching programme, i.e. sympathetic but intensive teaching. Others will reveal specific areas where gaps in development are holding them back, e.g. poor language development, lack of a satisfactory technique of word attack or weakness in comprehension. Such children need supplementary teaching to build up their weaker attributes. There will of course be a further group who have grave emotional problems or specific disabilities in the perceptual or linguistic fields and these should be referred for examination by an experienced remedial teacher and psychologist. Further stages of diagnostic observation will be necessary for these children but such work lies outside the scope of this book.

Stage 3

In order to set realistic objectives, it may be deemed necessary to undertake further testing and observation to establish in detail the child's needs. The following published diagnostic test material may be of help here.

1. Language difficulties. The following tests from the appendices to *The Language and Mental Development of Children* may prove helpful.
Vocabulary tests for young children
Words with more than one meaning
An English Language Scale
2. Visual, auditory and phonic skills. For children with a word recognition level below that of the average child of $6\frac{1}{2}$ years the

following tests from Daniels and Diack *Standard Reading Tests* may prove helpful.

Test 2. Copying abstract figures

Test 3. Copying a sentence

Test 4. Visual discrimination and orientation

Test 5. Letter recognition test

Test 6. Aural discrimination test

Test 7. Diagnostic word recognition test

For children whose reading is above the $6\frac{1}{2}$ years level but who have weaknesses in word recognition the following material from Schonell's *Backwardness in Basic Subjects* may prove helpful.

Test S4. Recall of three letter words—visual

Test S4. Recall of three letter words—aural

Test R5. Test of analysis and synthesis of common phonic units

Test R6. Test of directional attack on words

Test R7. Visual word discrimination test

For the teacher who has a group of children with word recognition difficulties, the following group test may be helpful and economic: C. Carver *Group Word Recognition Test* (ULP). The age norms given at 3-monthly intervals from 4 to $8\frac{1}{2}$ years. The test is untimed but takes approximately 30 minutes to administer. The teacher reads a given word and the children have to underline that word having selected it from a group of five words. A series of tests have been produced under the title *Phonic Survey* by S. Jackson and published by Gibson. This is a set of test sheets ranging from letter recognition to complex phonic words; each one takes approximately 5 minutes to administer. The teacher can select those tests which are felt to be appropriate to any given child and the handbook which accompanies the test material gives suggestions for treatment of various patterns of errors along the lines of a traditional phonic approach.

3. Objectives

Having assessed the needs, strengths and weaknesses of the child's reading ability, the point at which teaching can most effectively begin can be isolated. The programme designed for each individual child will follow these principles.

1. From the very beginning the child should achieve success or at least obtain a sense of success from activities in which he engages. This can be achieved by beginning at a level below his present attainment but using highly motivating material, by emphasizing his strengths or by guided reading in unison with a tape recorder.

2. The programme will aim to achieve progress through the child's strengths first and return to specific remediation for his weaknesses later.

3. Though there may well be a necessity for the development of skills in isolation this should always be matched with using reading for real purposes. Skill training will need to be undertaken in brief sessions and with the use of highly motivating materials. Games and machines can be most helpful here.

4. Every effort should be made to talk with the child about his difficulties and the work he is to undertake to overcome them.

5. The atmosphere should create the impression that reading can be enjoyable as well as useful.

6. Materials should be related to the interests and age of the child.

7. Diagnosis of needs should be a continuing feature of the work.

8. Reading attainment should not be gained at the expense of other areas otherwise it may well deteriorate when extra help ceases.

Further reading

ABLEWHITE, R. (1967) *The Slow Reader* Heinemann

DE HIRSCH, K. (1967) *Predicting Reading Failure* Harper and Row

MORRIS, J. M. (1966) *Standards and Progress in Reading* NFER

MOYLE, D. (1969) *Remedial Education* volume 4 no 2

MOYLE, D. (1970) *Special Education* June

MOYLE, D. and L. M. (1971) *Modern Innovations in the Teaching of Reading* ULP

STRANG, R. (1970 second edition) *The Diagnostic Teaching of Reading* McGraw-Hill

TANSLEY, A. E. (1967) *Reading and Remedial Teaching* Routledge and Kegan Paul

VERNON, M. D. (1971) *Reading and its Difficulties* CUP

CHAPTER 16

Reading standards considered

Teachers are usually very concerned to know whether or not the standard of reading among the children in their own class measures up favourably to that achieved by other children. Consequently reading tests are far more used by teachers than any other type of standardized testing materials. This concern is admirable, if it is in fact based in a desire to gain the best possible development in reading for the children. It is conceivable however that in our anxiety to produce measurable results such as excellent scores on a word recognition test we may not be providing the most helpful environment for the full all-round development of reading skill. In considering our reading standards therefore the level of performance in word recognition tests is only one factor, albeit an important one, among many. We must also view the level of proficiency achieved in comprehension, the extent of enjoyment in and the use of reading in out-of-school hours of a voluntary nature. This is necessary, for reading growth should continue after full-time education ceases and it will only do so if our young people continue to read. They will of course only continue to practise the skill if they gain enjoyment and value from it.

The extent of voluntary interest in reading, the amount actually read and the ability of adults to align their reading technique to the purpose of their reading are all very difficult to assess. One American survey suggests that only 18 per cent of American adults read books with any frequency whilst almost 50 per cent of British people do so. Even if this is true, the natural national pride which the statement occasions must be tempered with the question, 'Why do the other 50 per cent of our population not read regularly?' McMahan (1952) estimated that in the USA less than half the population ever read a book whilst only one-fifth ever bought a book. Public libraries in this country are more frequently used than ever before yet this extensive use comes from a very small percentage of the population, as low as 10 per cent in some areas. Again there is widespread criticism that the majority of our children who go on to follow courses in higher education have learned little concerning the use of books for study purposes.

Surveys of reading attainment were undertaken from 1948 to 1964 by the Ministry of Education and the Department of Education and Science. It is proposed to accept the figures from these surveys but the reader may well wish to inquire more deeply into their validity and for this purpose the various documents will be listed at the end of the chapter. The Ministry surveys were carried out on two age groups namely children of 11 and 15 years respectively. The test used was the Watts-Vernon test which has never been published and so the results of the tests are unaffected by practice. This test has 35 items and 10 minutes is allowed for its completion. The questions are of the multi-choice answer type and test both word recognition and comprehension.

Each of the four surveys made at intervals of four years since the first survey in 1948 has shown an increase in attainment over the previous survey. The improvement appears quite remarkable for the mean attainment of 11-year-old children in 1964 was 17 months higher than that of the same age group in 1948 and 23 months for children of 15 years over the same period. One item which seems to escape mention in recent reports however is that Vernon estimated that in 1948 the average attainment of children in reading at 11 years was 12 months and at 15 years 20 months below that of children of the same ages in 1939 due to the effects of the war. The tremendous advances claimed look very much less significant if viewed as 5 months over a period of 25 years. Gardner (1968) and Burt (1969) have both suggested that our reading standards, based on word recognition tests and to some lesser extent on tests of comprehension, are lower than they were in either of the periods immediately before the two great wars of this century.

An extensive survey by the National Foundation for Educational Research which took place during 1970-71 has recently been published. Though the differences in mean scores are not statistically significant there appears to be a slight drop in the average attainment in reading in comparison with the similar survey which the DES conducted in 1964. This is somewhat depressing for our schools have never been better equipped than they are today, interest in the teaching of reading has never been higher, innovation in methods of teaching and published materials has never been more extensive. It may be of course that the tests employed do not mirror the changes that have taken place in vocabulary on the one hand and curriculum on the other. Nevertheless our schools are still basing their curriculum on the assumption of literacy and whilst this remains so we must strive to gain higher standards and increased independence in reading for our children.

Surveys reported by Wiseman (1964) and Kellmer Pringle *et al* (1966) had suggested that there was an increase in the number of very good readers and a decrease in the number of children who were nonreaders or very poor readers. The 1971 NFER survey suggests however that though the mean scores of 11 and 15 year old children have fallen very minimally in comparison with 1964, the percentage of very good readers has fallen and the percentage of weak readers has grown. One must ask therefore whether the type of education provided for our children during the 1960s held sufficient challenge for the bright child, or gave enough attention to the needs of slower children and others who for some reason experienced difficulty in learning to read.

But what of the future? Might it be that the levels of attainment of children at present has reached the ceiling formed by their ability? This seems hardly credible when one examines all the evidence from research, the fact that human horizons and achievements seem to expand through the generations, and the very different levels of attainment in one school or class compared with another.

It appears fairly obvious that better levels of achievement are more likely to be achieved by the increased understanding, expertise and enthusiasm of teachers rather than innovations in methods and materials. Attention to the following areas might contribute significantly to an increase in achievement and the quality of the reading skill attained.

1. Reading teaching should be continued in some form throughout school life and existing approaches to beginning reading carefully reexamined in terms of the child's development into an effective, thoughtful and interested reader.
2. More extensive and enlightened training of all teachers in the reading process is necessary as also is the provision of advanced training so that every school may have a reading specialist upon its staff.
3. Despite the depressing evidence on class size, a reduction of class

size should be helpful, but only if teachers use the new opportunities given by smaller groups of children to the best advantage.

4. There should be a careful mixing of realistic and meaningful approach with a structured approach to reading. This can only be achieved when teachers are fully aware of the nature of the learning processes involved in reading.

In conclusion, the central role of reading in education cannot be overstressed. Not only is reading essential to the educative process and to human development generally, but reading and the way in which the child learns to read appear to have a marked effect upon the expansion of the ability to think. Any teacher of any subject at any level fails in his duty to the children if he does not provide some constructive help aimed at the extension and expansion of reading ability.

Further reading

BURT, C. (1969) in C. B. Cox and A. E. Dyson (Eds) *Black Paper Two* Critical Quarterly Society

DES (1966) *Progress in Reading* HMSO

GARDNER, W. K. (1968) in N. Smart (Ed) *Crisis in the Classroom* IPC

MORRIS, J. M. (1966) *Standards and Progress in Reading* NFER

KELLMER PRINGLE, M. L. (1966) *11,000 Seven Year Olds* Longmans

START, K. B. and WELLS, B. K. (1972) *The Trend of Reading Standards* NFER

STAUFFER, R. G. *Directing Reading Maturity as a Cognitive Process* Harper and Row

Attainment and diagnostic tests

Individual tests of reading attainment
Graded Word Reading Test C. Burt (ULP) 5 to 15 years
Graded Word Reading Test F. J. Schonell (Oliver and Boyd) 5 to 15 years
Graded Word Reading Test P. E. Vernon (ULP) 5 to 15 years
Simple Prose Reading Test F. J. Schonell (Oliver and Boyd) 5 to 9 years
Analysis of Reading Ability N. D. Neale (Macmillan) 6 to 14 years
Holborn Reading Scale A. F. Watts (Harrap) 6 to 14 years
Standard Reading Test 1 J. C. Daniels and H. Diack (Chatto and Windus) 5 to 9 years

Group tests of reading attainment
Group Reading Assessment F. A. Spooncer (ULP) 6 to 11 years
Group Reading Tests V. Southgate (ULP) 5 to 11 years
Group Reading Test D. Young (ULP) 7½ to 12½ years
Sentence Reading Test 1 A. F. Watts (NFER) 7½ to 11 years

Tests of comprehension
G.A.P. Reading Comprehension Test J. McLeod (Heinemann) 7½ to 12½ years
Secondary Reading Tests S. M. Bate (NFER) 11 to 15 years
Simple Prose Reading Test F. J. Schonell (Oliver and Boyd) 5 to 9 years
Silent Reading Tests A and B F. J. Schonell (Oliver and Boyd) 7 to 14 years
Analysis of Reading Ability M. D. Neale (Macmillan) 6 to 14 years
Manchester Reading Comprehension Test (Senior 1) S. Wiseman and Wrigley (ULP) 14 to 16 years

Diagnostic tests
Appendix to Backwardness in Basic Subjects F. J. Schonell (Oliver and Boyd)
Diagnostic Test of Word Recognition C. Carver (ULP)
Phonic Survey S. Jackson (Gibson)
The Standard Reading Tests J. C. Daniels and H. Diack (Chatto and Windus)
Reading and Remedial Reading A. E. Tansley (Routledge and Kegan Paul)

Some helpful American tests
Attainment and comprehension
Reading Tests A. I. Gates and W. H. MacGinitie (NFER)
SRA Reading Record G. T. Buswell (NFER)

Diagnostic
Doren Diagnostic Reading Tests G. Doren (NFER)
Durrell Analysis of Reading Difficulty D. D. Durrell (NFER)

Reading readiness
Harrison-Stroud Reading Profiles (NFER)
Reading Readiness Test A. I. Gates and W. H. MacGinitie (NFER)
Metropolitan Readiness Tests (NFER)

Reading schemes and materials

Reading schemes for infant schools

The Activity Reading Scheme E. R. Boyce (Macmillan 1956)

Beacon Readers J. H. Fassett *et al* (Ginn 1922, rev. 1965)

The Bluebird Series E. G. Davies (Chambers 1961)

Breakthrough to Literacy D. Mackay, B. Thompson, P. Schaub Schools Council Programme in Linguistics and English Teaching (Longmans 1970)

The Downing Reading Scheme (ita) J. Downing (Initial Teaching Publishing Company 1963)

Chapman Readers R. Bakewell and E. Wood (Chapman 1970)

Dominoes D. Glyn (Oliver and Boyd 1972)

Growing and Reading R. Bakewell and D. Fletcher (Macmillan 1956)

The Happy Trio Scheme W. S. Gray, M. Monroe, A. S. Artley (Pergamon 1962)

Happy Venture Reading Scheme—continued through the junior school in the *Wide Range* and *Reading On Series* F. J. Schonell (Oliver and Boyd 1939, rev. 1971)

Janet and John Readers M. O'Donnell and R. Munro—continued in the *Janet and John Extension Readers* (Nisbet 1949, rev. 1967)

Kathy and Mark M. O'Donnell and R. Munro (Nisbet 1969)

Ladybird Key Words Reading Scheme W. Murray (Wills and Hepworth 1964/72)

Let's Learn to Read J. Taylor and T. Ingleby (Blackie 1960)

McKee Readers and *Platform Readers* P. McKee, M. Lucille Harrison, A. McCowan, E. Lehr (Nelson 1959/72)

New Vanguard Readers P. Kettles and R. Macdonald (Holmes-McDougall 1963)

One, Two, Three and Away S. K. McCullagh (Hart-Davis 1964)

The Queensway Reading Scheme M. Brearley and L. Neilson (Evans 1964)

Ready to Read Scheme M. M. Simpson (Methuen 1966)

The Scott-Foresman Reading Systems H. Robinson *et al* (Scott-Foresman 1971)
Through the Rainbow E. Bradburne (Schofield and Sims 1964)
Time for Reading C. Obrist and P. Pickard (Ginn 1968)
Topsy and Sam D. J. Kirby (Cassell 1966)

There are of course many other excellent books for reading work in the infant school but the above have been selected because they are extensive in range and can be used from the very beginning of formal reading instruction.

Books to precede the reading scheme
Happy Trio Scheme 3 pre-readers (Pergamon 1956)
Getting Ready Book 1 in *McKee Readers Series*—see above (Nelson)
Getting Ready for Reading E. H. Grassam (Ginn 1949, rev. 1969)
Bluebird Picture Books Various authors (Chambers 1960)
New Age in Reading 4 books suitable for older children E. Clay (E. Arnold 1964)
Zero Books P. Usbourne (Macdonald Educational 1972)
Macmillan Colour Picture Books V. Southgate (Macmillan 1962)
New Colour Photo Books (E. J. Arnold 1948, rev. 1963)
Kenny Books (Philip and Tacey)
Ladybird Learning to Read Series Various authors (Wills and Hepworth 1956/72)
Early to Read A. E. Tansley and R. H. Nicholls (E. J. Arnold 1969/72)

Aids to word building
Apparatus
Clifton Audio-Visual Kit R. I. Brown and G. E. Bookbinder (ESA 1969)
English Colour Code Reading Programme D. V. Moseley (National Society for Mentally Handicapped Children, Centre for Learning Disabilities 1970)
Fun with Phonics M. Reis (Cambridge Art Publishers 1962)
Happy Words T. Kremer (Macdonald 1971)
Programmed Reading Kit D. H. Stott (Holmes 1962, rev. 1970)
Phonic Tapes and Workbooks (Remedial Supply Company, Dixon Street, Wolverhampton 1965)
Tackling New Words E. R. Boyce (ESA 1966)
Wordmaster Major M. Hardiment, J. Hicks and T. Kremer (Macdonald 1969)

Books

Over the Style M. Pitt Jones (A. and C. Black 1961)
Sounds and Words V. Southgate and F. Havenhand (ULP 1960)
Sound Sense A. E. Tansley now has matched tapes (E. J. Arnold 1960)
Learn Your Sounds J. Taylor and T. Ingleby (Blackie 1963)
Sounding and Blending J. A. Willsdon (Gibson 1967)

Reading schemes with a phonic bias

Basic Reading Series D. Rasmussen and L. Goldberg (SRA 1964)
Colour Story Reading J. K. Jones (Nelson 1967)
Gay Way Reading Scheme E. R. Boyce (Macmillan 1950)
Programmed Reading C. D. Buchanan (Sullivan Associates 1963)
Royal Road Readers J. C. Daniels and H. Diack (Chatto and Windus 1956, rev. 1971)
Step Up and Read W. R. Jones (ULP 1965)
Words in Colour C. Gattegno (Educational Explorers 1962)

Books suitable for remedial work

Active Reading Scheme J. E. Miles (Ginn 1959)
An extensive scheme of readers for the secondary school child. The first three books have large workbooks and reading games to accompany them. Reading age of first three books 6 to 9 years.
Adventures in Life R. H. Jones and H. Saltiel (Wheaton 1962)
16 readers with accompanying workbooks of a phonic nature— 8 for boys, 8 for girls. Reading age 7½ to 9 years. Interest age 9 to 14 years.
Ann and Jenny Books A. Boyers (Ginn 1965)
Readers for girls at the top end of the secondary school. Reading age 9 plus years.
Anvil Books K. Rudge (Hamish Hamilton 1960)
16 books. Reading age 7 to 8 years. Interest age 9 to 13 years.
Burgess Readers C. V. Burgess (ULP 1961)
8 books with workbooks and playlets. Reading age 8 to 9½ years. Interest age 10 to 14 years.
Bandit Books Various authors (Ernest Benn 1963)
Full length books of adult appearance for secondary school children. Reading age 9 plus.
Beginning to Read Books Various authors (Ernest Benn 1966/67)
12 books. Reading age 6 to 7 years. Interest age 7 to 10 years.
Booster Books W. C. H. Chalk (Heinemann 1965)
10 books with accompanying workbooks. Reading age 7½ to 9 years. Interest age 11 to 15 years.

Challenge Readers C. Niven (McDougall 1963)
8 books. Reading age 6 to 9 years. Interest age 9 to 12 years.
Cowboy Sam Series E. Chandler (E. J. Arnold 1963)
9 books. Reading age 6½ to 8 years. Interest age 7 to 11 years.
Data Books P. Young (Schofield and Sims 1966)
Books and workbooks of unusual format Reading age 7 to 9.
Interest age 9 to 13.
Far and Near Books Various authors (Chambers 1965)
26 books. Reading age 7 to 9 years. Interest age 10 to 15 years.
Good Company Readers A. Elliott-Cannon (Johnston and Bacon 1967)
8 books with matching development books Reading age 7 to 13
years. Interest age 9 to 15 years.
The Go Readers M. Calman (Blond 1964)
4 books. Reading age 6 to 7½ years. Interest age 9 to 13 years.
The Griffin Readers S. K. McCullagh (E. J. Arnold 1959)
12 readers forming one complete story. *Dragon Books* have been
added which can be used as supplementary reading or as a scheme
on its own. 6 workbooks. 4 pre-readers. Reading age 6 to 8 years.
Interest age 8 to 14 years.
The Holly Adventures K. Rudge (Hamish Hamilton 1961)
4 books. Reading age 8 to 9 years. Interest age 10 to 14 girls.
Inner Ring Books A. Pullen and C. Rapstoff (Ernest Benn 1965)
12 books. Reading age 7 plus years. Interest age 11 to 15 years.
Jet Books Various authors (Cape 1963)
12 books in modern paperback style. Reading age 9 plus years.
Interest age 11 to 15 years.
Joan Tate Books Joan Tate (Heinemann 1966)
18 books. Reading age 9 plus. Interest age 12 plus years.
Ladybird Key Words Reading Scheme W. Murray (Wills and Hep-
    worth 1964)
12 stages with 3 books to each stage. The C series includes written
and phonic work. Reading age 5 to 9 years. Interest age 5 to 11
years.
Micky Books D. H. Stott (Holmes 1964)
4 books. Reading age 8 to 9½ years. Interest age 9 to 14 years.
Mike and Mandy Readers M. Durward (Nelson 1956)
12 books with written and phonic exercises at the end of each book.
Reading age 6 to 8½ years. Interest age 8 to 12 years.
Modern Reading G. Keir (ULP 1963)
6 books with matching workbooks. Reading age 6 to 8 years.
Interest age 10 to 14 years.

The New Age in Reading E. Clay (E. Arnold 1964)
4 pre-readers, 6 sets of 6 readers covering a reading age range of
5 to 10 years. Interest age 8 to 14 years.
Nippers Edited by L. Berg (Macmillan 1969)
Reading age 7 to 8. Interest age 7 to 11 years.
Oxford Colour Books C. Carver and C. H. Stowasser (OUP 1963)
More than 30 titles, each book containing puzzles and suggested
written work. Some workbooks which can be used with the
scheme are now available. Reading age 6 to 9 years. Interest age
8 to 13 years.
Racing to Read A. E. Tansley and R. H. Nicholls (E. J. Arnold 1962,
   rev. 1970)
21 books. Reading age 5 to $7\frac{1}{2}$ years. Interest age 7 to 11 years.
Rescue Reading J. Webster (Ginn 1968)
18 books, workbooks, programme pads and activity books. The
scheme includes many helpful reading activities. Reading age 6 to 9
years. Interest age 7 to 13 years.
Sea Hawk Series S. K. McCullagh (E. J. Arnold 1965)
Tales of the sea for secondary school children. Reading age 6 to 8
years.
Simon and Dorothy Readers P. Emmens (Blond 1963)
Reading age 8 to 10 years. Interest age 10 to 14 years.
Spotlight on Trouble Series H. G. Gunzburg (Methuen 1965)
Reading age 8 to 10 years. Interest age 14 plus years.
Step Up and Read W. R. Jones (ULP 1965)
Phonic cards, 6 readers, 3 workbooks. Reading age 6 to $8\frac{1}{2}$ years.
Interest age 9 to 13 years.
Swift Readers T. Elder and R. Wood (Harrap 1964)
Good stories with comprehension work. Reading age 7 to 11 years.
Interest age 9 to 14 years.
Teenage Twelve S. Richardson, D. Whitehouse and G. Wilkinson
   (Gibson 1966)
12 readers based on the Dolch word list. Reading age 7 plus years.
Interest age 9 to 13 years.
Tempo Books P. Groves and L. Stratta (Longmans 1966)
10 books. Reading age $6\frac{1}{2}$ to $8\frac{1}{2}$ years. Interest age 9 to 13 years.
Tim's Gang D. J. Kirby (Hamish Hamilton 1967)
4 books. Reading age 6 to 7 years. Interest age 9 to 13 years.
Titan Books Various authors (Ward Lock Educational 1967)
4 books. Reading age 9 plus years. Interest age 13 plus years.
True Adventure Series E. Jerome (Blackie 1959)

More than 30 titles. Reading age 8 plus years. Interest age 9 to 14 years.

Websters of Welford J. C. Uncles (Nelson 1964)
5 books. Reading age 7 to 8 years. Interest age 9 to 13 years.

Windrush Books Various authors (OUP 1963)
8 books. Reading age 9 years. Interest age 10 to 13 years.

Working World Series Various authors (Cassell 1965)
A four-year course of study in all subjects for secondary school children, graded for reading age

Further detailed information on reading schemes and materials will be found in K. S. Lawson *Children's Reading* (University of Leeds Institute of Education 1968). The Centre for the Teaching of Reading, 29 Eastern Avenue, Reading, Berkshire, produces lists of reading materials and tests which are regularly updated.

Bibliography

ABLEWHITE, R. (1967) *The Slow Reader* Heinemann
AUSUBEL, R. (1963) *The Psychology of Meaningful Verbal Learning* Greene and Stratton
BENNETT, S. M. (1951) *British Journal of Educational Psychology* 21
BENTON, A. L. (1962) in J. Money (Ed) *Reading Disability* J. Hopkins Press
BERNSTEIN, B. (1961) *Educational Research* Volume 3, no. 3
BIRCH, H. E. (1962) in J. Money (Ed) *Reading Disability* J. Hopkins Press
BLIESMER, E. P. (1954) *Journal of Educational Psychology* 45
BLOOMFIELD, L. and BARNHARDT, C. (1961) *Let's Read* Wayne State University Press
BOWDEN, J. H. (1911) *Elementary School Teacher* 12
BRIMER, M. A. (1967) in W. D. Wall (Ed) *New Research in Education* NFER
BROWN, A. L. (1967) (Ed) *Reading: Current Research and Practice* Chambers
BRUCKNER, M. D. (1954) *Catholic Educational Review* 52
BUROS, O. K. (1968) *Reading Tests and Reviews* Gryphon Press
BURT, C. (1937) *The Backward Child* ULP
BURT, C. and LEWIS, R. B. (1946) *British Journal of Educational Psychology* 16
BURT, C. (1969) in C. B. Cox and A. E. Dyson (Eds) *Black Paper Two* Critical Quarterly Society
BUSWELL, G. T. (1922) *Supplementary Educational Mono* 21 Chicago
CANE, B. and SMITHERS, J. (1971) *The Roots of Reading* NFER
CHALL, J. (1967) *Learning to Read: The Great Debate* McGraw-Hill
CHAMBERS, A. (1969) *The Reluctant Reader* Pergamon
CLARK, M. M. (1970) *Reading Difficulty in Schools* Penguin
COHEN, S. A. (1969) *Teach Them All to Read* Random House
COLLINS, C. E. (1961) *The Effects of Remedial Teaching* Educational Mono 4 University of Birmingham

CONDUCT, G. N. and WARD, H. (1955) Phonic reading—a new approach in *Educational Review* 7

CROOKES, T. J. and GREENE, M. C. L. (1963) *British Journal of Educational Psychology* 33

DALE, N. (1899) *On the Teaching of English Reading* Philip

DANIELS, J. C. and DIACK, H. (1956) *Progress in Reading* University of Nottingham

DANIELS, J. C. and DIACK, H. (1958) *Progress in Reading in the Infants School* University of Nottingham

DANIELS, J. C. and DIACK, H. (1958) *The Standard Reading Tests* Chatto and Windus

DAVIDSON, H. P. (1931) *Genetic Psychology Mono* 9

DAVIE, R., BUTLER, N. R. and GOLDSTEIN, H. (1972) *From Birth to Seven* Longman

DEARBORN, W. F. (1936) *Psychological Mono* 47 no. 2

DE HIRSCH, K. (1967) *Predicting Reading Failure* Harper and Row

DE LEEUW, E. and M. (1965) *Read Better, Read Faster* Penguin

DEPARTMENT OF EDUCATION AND SCIENCE (1966) *Progress in Reading* HMSO

DIACK, H. (1960) *Reading and the Psychology of Perception* P. Skinner

DIACK, H. (1965) *In Spite of the Alphabet* Chatto and Windus

DOLCH, E. W. (1948) *Problems in Reading* Garrard Press

DOLCH, E. W. and BLOOMSTER (1937) *Elementary School Journal*

DOMAN, G. (1963) *Teach Your Baby to Read* Jonathan Cape

DOWNING, J. A. (1964) *The ita Reading Experiment* Evans

DOWNING, J. A. and JONES, J. K. (1966) *Educational Research* February

DOWNING, J. A. (1966) *The First International Reading Symposium* Cassell

DOWNING, J. A. and THACKRAY, D. V. (1971) *Reading Readiness* ULP

DUNCAN, J. (1940) *Backwardness in Reading* Harrap

DURKIN, D. (1964) *Reading Teacher* 18

DURRELL, D. D. (1940) *The Improvement of Basic Reading Abilities* World Book Company

DURRELL, D. D. (1956) *Improving Reading Instruction* Harcourt, Brace and World

EDWARDS, R. P. A. and GIBBON, V. (1964) *Words Your Children Use* Burke

FARNHAM, A. B. (1965) quoted by Smith in *American Reading Instruction* IRA

FARR, R. and ANASTASIOW, N. (1969) *Tests of Reading Readiness and Achievement* IRA

FERNALD,H. B. and KELLER,G. (1921) *Journal of Educational Research* 4

FLESCH, R. (1955) *Why Johnny Can't Read* Harper

FLETCHER, H. (1953) *Speech and Hearing in Communication* Van Nostrand

FRANK, H. (1935) *British Journal of Educational Psychology* 5

FRIES, C. C. (1962) *Linguistics and Reading* Holt, Rinehart and Winston

GARDNER, D. E. M. (1966) *Experiment and Tradition in Primary Schools* Methuen

GARDNER, W. K. (1965) *Towards Literacy* Blackwell

GARDNER, W. K. (Ed) (1970) *Reading Skills: Theory and Practice* Ward Lock Educational

GATES, A. I. (1930) *Interest and Ability in Reading* Macmillan

GATES, A. I. (1937) *Elementary School Journal* 37

GATES, A. I. (1939) *Elementary School Journal* 39

GATES, A. I. and BOEKER (1923) *Teachers' College Record* 24

GATES, A. I. and RUSSELL (1938) *Elementary School Journal* 39

GATTEGNO, C. (1962) *Words in Colour* Educational Explorers

GESELL, A. and ILG, F. (1946) *The Child from Five to Ten* Hamish Hamilton

GILLILAND, J. (1972) *Readability* ULP

GODDARD, N. L. (1962) *Reading in the Modern Infants School* ULP

GOODACRE, E. J. (1967) *Reading in Infant Classes* NFER

GOODACRE, E. J. (1971) *Children and Learning to Read* Routledge and Kegan Paul

GOODMAN, K. S. (1969) Analysis of oral reading miscues: applied psycholinguistics in *Reading Research Quarterly* 5

GRAY, W. S. (1937) *Second Report of the National Committee on Reading*

GULLIFORD, R. (1967) Lecture to a Conference at Edge Hill College of Education

HEBB, D. O. (1949) *The Organization of Human Behaviour* Chapman and Hall

HILDRETH, F. (1932) *Child Development* 3

HOLMES, J. A. (1962) in *Challenge and Experiment in Reading* Scholastic Magazine

HOUGHTON and DANIELS J. C., (1966) *Bulletin of the United Kingdom Reading Association*

HUGHES, J. M. (1971) *Aids to Reading* Evans

HYMES, J. L. (1958) *Before the Child Reads* Row, Peterson

ILG, F. and AMES,L. B. (1950) *Journal of Genetic Psychology* 76

INGLIS, W. B. (1948) in *Studies in Reading: Volume 1* ULP

JACKSON, S. (1967) *The Teacher's Guide to Tests and Testing* Longmans

JAGGER, J. H. (1929) *The Sentence Method of Teaching Reading* Grant

JONES, J. K. (1964) *British Journal of Educational Psychology* 34

KEIR, G. (1951) *Teacher's Companion to Adventures in Reading* ULP

KELLMER PRINGLE, M. L. (1961) *Educational Research* 4

KELLMER PRINGLE, M. L., BUTLER, N. R. and DAVIE, R. (1966) *11,000 Seven Year Olds* Longmans

KENNEDY (1942) *Journal of Experimental Education* 10

KIRK, S. A. and JOHNSON, G. O. (1951) *Educating the Retarded Child* Houghton Mifflin

KOPEL, D. (1942) *Teacher's College Journal* 13

LATHAM, D. (1971) *Six Reading Schemes and their Interchangeability* Cambridge Institute of Education

LEE, T. (1967) in A. L. Brown (Ed) *Reading: Current Research and Practice* Chambers

LEEDHAM, J. and UNWIN, D. (1965) *Programmed Learning in School* Longmans

LEFEVRE, C. (1964) *Linguistics and the Teaching of Reading* McGraw-Hill

LEWIS, M. M. (1962) *Language and Thought and Personality in Infancy and Childhood* ULP

LUNZER, E. A. and MORRIS, J. F. (1968) *Development in Learning* volume 2 *Development in Human Learning* Staples

LOVELL, K. (1963) *British Journal of Educational Psychology* 33

LYNN, R. (1963) *Educational Research* 6

MACKAY, D., THOMPSON, B. and SCHAUB, P. (1970) *Breakthrough to Literacy: Teacher's Manual* Longmans

MADISON, L. (1956) *Perceptual Motor Skills* 6

MALMQUIST, E. (1958) *Reading Disabilities in the First Grade of the Elementary School* Almquist and Wiksell

MATHEWS, M. M. (1966) *Teaching to Read* University of Chicago Press

McDADE, J. E. (1937) *Journal of Educational Research* 30

McLATCHEY (1946) *Educational Research Bulletin* 25

McMAHAN, A. (1952) in *The Wonderful World of Books* New American Library of World Literature

McMANUS, A. (1964) *Reading Teaching* 18

McNALLY, J. and MURRAY, W. (1962) *Key Words to Literacy* Schoolmaster

MERRITT, J. E. (1971) (Ed) *Reading and the Curriculum* Ward Lock Educational

MIDGELEY, J. D. (1952) Report to the Medical Research Council

MILLS, R. E. (1955) *Learning Methods Test* Fort Lauderdale Mills Centre

MINISTRY OF EDUCATION (1950) *Reading Ability* Pamphlet 18

MORPHETT, M. V. and WASHBURNE, C. (1931) *Elementary School Journal* 31

MORRIS, J. M. (1966) *Standards and Progress in Reading* NFER

MORRIS, R. (1963) *Success and Failure in Learning to Read* Oldbourne

MOXON, C. A. V. (1962) *A Remedial Reading Method* Methuen

MOYLE, D. (1966) *Bulletin of the United Kingdom Reading Association*

MOYLE, D. (1969) *Everyweek Teachers' Bulletin* spring no. 9, summer no. 7

MOYLE, D. (1969) *Remedial Education* volume 4, no. 2

MOYLE, D. and MOYLE, L. M. (1971) *Modern Innovations in Reading Teaching* ULP

MURPHY, M. L. (1966) *Creative Writing* Educational Explorers

MURPHY, M. L. (1968) *Douglas Can't Read* Educational Explorers

MURRAY, W. (1969) *Teaching Reading* Wills and Hepworth

NAESLAND, J. (1955) *Research Bulletin* no. 4 University of Stockholm

NEWSON, E. (1955) *Unpublished thesis* Nottingham University

OLSON, W. (1959) *Child Development* Heath

PARKER, D. H. (1958) *Schooling for Individual Excellence* Nelson

PITMAN, J. and ST JOHN, J. (1969) *Alphabets and Reading* Pitman

PONT, H. B. (1966) An investigation into the use of the SRA Reading Laboratory in three Midlothian Schools in *Educational Research* June

POTTER, M. C. (1940) *Teachers' College Contributions to Education* 939

PRESTON, M. I. (1939) *Child Development* 10

RAVENNETTE, A. T. (1969) *Dimensions of Reading Difficulty* Pergamon

REID, J. F. (1970) *Research in Education*

RICKARD, C. E. (1935) *Journal of Educational Research* 29

ROBERTS, G. R. (1969) *Reading in Primary Schools* Routledge and Kegan Paul

ROBINSON, F. P. (1960) *Effective Study* Harper

ROBINSON, H. M. (1968) (Ed) *Innovation and Change in Reading Instruction* NSSE

ROBINSON, H. M. (1966) in J. Downing (Ed) *First International Reading Symposium* Cassell

ROSWELL, F. and NATCHEZ, G. (1964) *Reading Disability* Basic Books

RUSSELL, D. A. and KARP, E. E. (1951) *Reading Aids Through the Grades* Columbia University

SCHONELL, F. J. (1940) *British Journal of Educational Psychology* 10

SCHONELL, F. J. (1942) *Backwardness in Basic Subjects* Oliver and Boyd

SCHONELL, F. J. (1945) *The Psychology and Teaching of Reading* Oliver and Boyd

SCHONELL, F. J. (1949) *British Journal of Educational Psychology* 19

SMITH, F. (1971) *Understanding Reading* Holt, Rinehart and Winston

SMITH, M. E. (1926) *An Investigation into the Development of the Sentence and Extent of Vocabulary in Young Children* University of Iowa

SMITH, N. B. (1966) in J. Downing (Ed) *First International Reading Symposium* Cassell

SMITH, N. B. (1965) *American Reading Instruction* IRA

SOUTHGATE, V. (1972) *Beginning Reading* ULP

SOUTHGATE, V. and ROBERTS, G. R. (1970) *Reading: Which Approach?* ULP

START, K. B. and WELLS, B. K. (1972) *The Trend of Reading Standards* NFER

STAUFFER, R. G. (1969) *Learning to Read as a Thinking Process* Harper and Row

STAUFFER, R. G. (1970) *Directing Reading Maturity as a Cognitive Process* Harper and Row

STAUFFER, R. G. (1970) *The Language Experience Approach to the Teaching of Reading* Harper and Row

STOTT, D. H. (1964) *Roads to Literacy* Holmes

STRANG, R. (1970) *The Diagnostic Teaching of Reading* McGraw-Hill

TANSLEY, A. E. (1967) *Reading and Remedial Reading* Routledge and Kegan Paul

TATE, H. L. (1937) *Elementary School Journal* 37

TAYLOR, C. D. (1950) *Studies in Reading* ULP

THACKRAY, D. V. (1972) *Readiness for Reading* Chapman

VERNON, M. D. (1957) *Backwardness in Reading* CUP

VERNON, M. D. (1972) *Reading and its Difficulties* CUP

VERNON, P. E. (1948) *Measurement of Abilities* ULP

VERNON, P. E. (1956) *The Measurement of Abilities* ULP

VILSCEK, E. (1968) (Ed) *A Decade of Innovations* IRA

VYGOTSKY, L. S. (1962) *Thought and Language* MIT Press

WALL, W. D. (1945 and 1946) *British Journal of Educational Psychology* 15, 16

WALL, W. D. (1967) (Ed) *New Research in Education* NFER

WARBURTON, F. W. and SOUTHGATE, V. (1969) *ita: An Independent Evaluation* Murray and Chambers

WARDHAUGH, R. (1969) *Reading: A Linguistic Perspective* Harcourt, Brace and World

WATTS, A. F. (1944) *The Language and Mental Development of Children* Harrap

WEBSTER, J. (1965) *Practical Reading* Evans

WILEY, W. E. (1928) *Journal of Educational Research* 17

WILKINSON, A. (1971) *The Foundations of Language* OUP

WILSON, F. T. and FLEMMING, C. W. (1938) *Journal of Genetic Psychology* 53

WISEMAN, S. (1964) *Education and Environment* MUP

WOODROW, H. (1945) *Journal of Educational Psychology* 36

YEDINACK, J. G. (1949) *Journal of Genetic Psychology* 74

Index

Note: Only those reading schemes, tests and materials have been indexed which are referred to in the main text of the book. Many others are listed in Appendixes 1 — tests (pages 220–1) and 2 — reading schemes and materials (pages 222–7).